KU-725-696

ROBIN PEDLEY

The Comprehensive School

PENGUIN BOOKS

Penguin Books Ltd, Harmondsworth, Middlesex
U.S.A.: Penguin Books Inc., 3300 Clipper Mill Road, Baltimore 11, Md
AUSTRALIA: Penguin Books Pty Ltd, 762 Whitehorse Road,
Mitcham, Victoria

—

First published 1963

—

Copyright © Robin Pedley, 1963

—

Made and printed in Great Britain
by C. Nicholls & Company Ltd
Set in Linotype Pilgrim

Contents

Author's Note

MY subject is the comprehensive school in England, Wales, and the Isle of Man. A study of schools of similar type in other parts of the world would fill many volumes, and I have therefore looked elsewhere only for occasional illustration and comparison.

I have not included Scotland in this study, because that country has its own educational system, different from ours both in tradition and in structure. There are certain parallels: the 'omnibus' schools of the Scottish countryside are not unlike our rural comprehensive schools, the large new comprehensive schools of Glasgow resemble some of those on the fringe of our big cities, and Fife has recently introduced a 'two-tier' system of junior and senior high schools similar to that which, in different forms, is at last beginning to find favour here. To Scotland, too, we owe the mixed blessing of much assiduous work in the measurement of ability; and many of our local education authorities still rely on Edinburgh's college of education, Moray House, for the intelligence tests they use in the eleven-plus examination.

Where both similarities and radical differences exist, however, as they do between Scotland and England, a composite picture is likely to be too confusing. The Scottish scene is best described separately.

Acknowledgements

I AM indebted, first of all, to the many head teachers and education officers who in countless ways have helped my study of secondary education during the past ten years. I wish particularly to record my appreciation of the generosity of the Protestant School Board of Greater Montreal, and of many Canadian friends, whose invitations made possible my study of Canadian schools and teacher training at first hand. I have greatly benefited, too, from the frequent exchange of critical ideas with parents, teachers, lay members of education committees, university scholars, and others – especially those whose views have differed from mine.

Professor and Mrs J. W. Tibble have long been major influences in helping me to shape my own educational philosophy. Their constant friendship, inspiration, and encouragement defy valuation. Mr Brian Simon's scholarship has been an immense resource, and I thank him for many helpful suggestions. My brothers, Mr W. H. Pedley and Mr F. H. Pedley, have given important criticism and advice.

I thank the London County Council for permission to include three tables from its recent publication, *London Comprehensive Schools*, and the responsible editors who have kindly permitted me to reproduce parts of the following essays: 'Comprehensive Schools Today' (Councils & Education Press, 1955), 'Lessons from Canada' (*Education*, 3 July 1959), 'The Choice before us: alternatives to 11+' (*The Times Educational Supplement*, 6 February 1959), and 'Quest for Quality' (*ibid.*, 24 March 1961). I am grateful, too, for the help given to me by the Research Board of the University of Leicester, and for the prompt response of the statistics branch of the Ministry of Education to my periodic requests for factual information.

1. 'A New Society'?

'IN spite of the virtual abolition of poverty, in spite of the rise there has been in the rewards of labour, in spite of the fact that . . . the great bulk of the nation now regards itself as middle-class, Britain is still a jealous and divided nation.'[1]

England in the 1960s is an aristocratic society, not a democratic one. That is the main fact to be realized if its system of education is to be fully understood. The majority of its citizens still believe in aristocracy (government by the best people) rather than in democracy (government by all the people).

At one time it was assumed that quality went with noble birth. Then wealth replaced birth as the *sine qua non*. Both criteria live on in English society today, but ability is rapidly replacing them as the key to a position of power. Because the term 'aristocracy' has become entangled in people's minds with the idea of an unjustly privileged class, the word 'meritocracy' has recently been coined to express more clearly the new system of government by the ablest people. The Englishman of the 1960s does not believe in equality. What he wants is equal opportunity to be unequal.

We have, then, a society made up of different classes. Because many top people still owe their eminence to birth and inherited wealth, now increasingly felt to be 'unfair', there is much pressure to reform the conditions of membership, making personal ability the measuring-rod, and to ease movement from one class to another. Such reforms will of course strengthen the class system. They are completely at variance with the quite different aim of a minority of idealists: to abolish the class system altogether.

1. *The Times*, leading article of 13 July 1961, 'A New Society'.

Education in England mirrors the English social system. There are three main routes through early life, each with its social ranking order. Transfer from one route to another can occur in special cases, and the possibility of such transfer acts as a social safety valve; but a child launched on the second or third route must combine marked ability with good fortune, if he is not to follow that track to the end. For those interested in athletics these routes may be likened to the lanes in which the 400 metres is run, with one vital exception: there is no staggered start to ensure an equal chance for all competitors.

Route One, normally open to the children of parents who can afford to pay large fees, takes a boy from private kindergarten (perhaps four to eight) to preparatory school (eight to thirteen), 'public' or independent school (thirteen to eighteen), and, provided he has the modest ability required to matriculate, Oxford University or Cambridge University. Of all fourteen-year-olds in England and Wales, six per cent are on the inside lane: four per cent in recognized independent schools, two per cent in direct-grant grammar schools.

The latter are independent of local authorities, but receive a grant direct from the Ministry of Education. In addition to fee-payers, they must take at least twenty-five per cent of their pupils from local primary schools; these pupils are selected on the results of the eleven-plus examination. There are only 178 direct-grant grammar schools in England and Wales.

The leading 'public' schools now set quite exacting entrance tests for nearly all their pupils – a further sign that ability is slowly coming to be the first requirement for membership of the top social group. Likewise, at Oxford and Cambridge, severe competition from brilliant grammar school pupils limits the number of places which may be quietly reserved for the ordinary scions of famous fathers.

Even so, longstanding personal contacts among particular colleges and 'public' and preparatory schools still ensure that the requirement of great academic ability, demanded of most applicants, may be remitted in favoured cases. The experience of Winston Churchill over seventy years ago is not wholly out of date. This is his own account of an examination he sat for admission to a famous independent school.

I wrote my name at the top of the page. I put down the number of the question: '1'. After much reflection I put a bracket round it thus: '(1)'. But thereafter I could not think of anything connected with it that was either relevant or true. Incidentally there arrived from nowhere in particular a blot and several smudges. I gazed for two whole hours at this sad spectacle: and then merciful ushers collected my piece of foolscap with all the others and carried it up to the Headmaster's table. It was from these slender indications of scholarship that Mr Welldon drew the conclusion that I was worthy to pass into Harrow.[1]

Route Two is much more conditioned by the new accent on ability, though not wholly so. Twenty-four per cent of each age group are in this middle lane – seventeen per cent in local grammar schools, three per cent in technical schools, and four per cent in comprehensive schools. It normally takes a boy from the local primary school to the grammar school after passing the eleven-plus qualifying examination, and thence, after eventually gaining two or three advanced-level passes in the General Certificate of Education (GCE), to a provincial university. A brilliant minority force their way into Oxford or Cambridge. Others may go to a technical college or direct into commerce or industry. The successful local grammar-school boy's normal target, however, is coming to be a place at a provincial university; and as more of these places are provided, as industry requires more educated personnel, and as therefore

1. *My Early Life* (Odhams Press, 1934).

more boys and girls stay at school until eighteen to prepare for full-time education, it will increasingly be so.

Route Three is mainly for those who fail to qualify for a grammar school at eleven: sixty-six per cent in 'secondary modern', other secondary, and all-age schools, two per cent in other independent schools, and one per cent in special schools.[1] Most go to 'modern' schools and normally leave at fifteen or sixteen. In some of the 3900 'modern' schools in England and Wales it is possible for the cleverer pupils to sit for GCE at ordinary level, and many more take examinations at a lower level. A minority go on to gain a technical college qualification by long and arduous part-time study. The vast majority, however, become the hewers of wood and drawers of water of our graded society. A Certificate of Secondary Education is to be instituted for those pupils who are unable to take GCE. This new certificate will further refine the educational ranking order.

This, of course, is an over-simplified picture. Not all boys from independent schools go to Oxford or Cambridge, and far fewer girls; for women are only grudgingly accepted in those very conservative communities. An increasing number of very able grammar-school pupils are entering Oxford and Cambridge. On the other hand, there is little chance to move from the middle to the inside lane at any earlier stage. At the other end of the scale it is possible for a few 'modern' school children to secure transfer to the grammar school at thirteen or sixteen, and the odd one may even reach a provincial university.

Such exceptions blur the hard outlines of a three-class system of education. They are necessary to make such a system tolerable. They provide escape channels for the exceptionally able, but they do not seriously alter the

1. 6% (route 1) + 24% (route 2) + 69% (route 3) = 99%. Small fractions, omitted in calculating to the nearest whole number, account for the missing 1%.

main pattern; rather do they help to entrench it further. As the editor of *School and College* forthrightly states: 'The whole issue is one of class ... for the English, more than others, believe in class and have taken the greatest pains to establish and protect it.'[1]

In his novel about the Civil Service in England, *Clerks in Lowly Orders*, Stuart Mitchell states Plato's ideas in modern terms. There are the men of gold, the administrative class who decide policy, drawn almost exclusively from the runners on the inside lane. There are the men of silver, the executive class, who interpret and implement that policy, drawn from those who have followed the less advantageous middle lane. And there are the men of brass, the clerical class who do the routine work, who have hopelessly followed the outside lane in the educational race. The proposed new Certificate of Secondary Education, open to such people, will make a last careful distinction between the men of brass and the men of dross: a timely incentive, this, to encourage the upward struggle among even the lowliest of us.

At present we are doing little to put an end to the advantages held by those who occupy the inside lane. The great argument in England, curiously enough, is almost entirely about the desirability of removing the line between the middle and the outside lanes which is drawn from the age of eleven onwards, and which depends on the most celebrated, most unpopular, yet most potent feature of English education – the eleven-plus examination.

Selection at eleven[2]

The eleven-plus examination is a process of selection for

1. *School and College*, February 1962, p. 13.
2. The best general survey of this subject is *Secondary School Selection*, ed. Vernon, the report of a British Psychological Society inquiry (Methuen, 1957).

places in grammar schools, and sometimes technical schools, which may take anything from three months to three years to complete. At its best it is perhaps the most thorough examination ever devised, and it is usually administered with meticulous fairness. It normally consists of four parts: (i) tests of intelligence; (ii) tests of attainment in English and Arithmetic; (iii) records of the child's work at primary school with teachers' recommendations; (iv) interviews, in borderline cases.

Intelligence tests produce a rating called the intelligence quotient, or I.Q. This is the child's mental age, as measured by the tests, expressed as a percentage of chronological age. Thus a child of ten whose mental age is twelve has an I.Q. of 120. A child of ten whose mental age is eight has an I.Q. of 80.

The proportion of children admitted to a grammar school varies according to the number of places available and the policy of the local education authority. It may be as low as ten per cent or as high as forty per cent of all the children for whom the local education authority is responsible. (Fee-payers at independent and direct-grant schools are excluded from these calculations.) The average for England and Wales is twenty per cent. Children with I.Q.s of 120 and over usually qualify for places in grammar schools.

Before 1955 or thereabouts, public confidence in the fairness and accuracy of the examination rested on the belief that intelligence tests could detect and measure inborn ability. In the middle fifties this belief was strongly challenged by such university teachers as Philip Vernon, Brian Simon, and John Daniels, who demonstrated conclusively that this was not so. None of the tests conceived and tried over the course of sixty years can satisfactorily distinguish natural talent from what has been learned. Heredity and environment are too closely entangled to be closely identified. This means that children from literate homes, with interested and helpful parents, have an enormous advantage over children from culturally poor homes where books are unknown and conversation is either limited or unprintable.

Children's attainment in English and mathematics is also greatly affected by such factors. Some parents spend hours helping their children to read. At the other extreme, there are parents who violently prevent their children from reading; in such homes books are hated or despised. Many parents are indifferent. Further, progress is much affected by health, attendance at school, and the luck of having a good or a bad class teacher there.

Surveys indicate that teachers' reports, taken as a whole, are just as valid as intelligence tests. But here too much depends on the judgement of individuals; one teacher's may be very good, another's poor. The intelligence test is more uniform and stable. Moreover the responsibility of deciding whether a child goes to the grammar school or not is one which few teachers relish. They know how fallible the available evidence must often be, how unpredictable the response of children to future stimuli.

Teachers' judgements may seem to be better than they really are, because grouping in the junior school itself helps to decide a child's success or failure at eleven-plus. 'Give a dog a bad name' is all too pertinent here. A child put in the 'A' or top stream at the age of seven finds himself in a stimulating environment. He is often also given one of the better teachers. Such a child may reasonably be expected to go on doing well and be selected for a grammar school. Conversely the child labelled 'C' at seven, in a much less stimulating environment, feeling inferior, and not infrequently put in the care of a poorer teacher, has little chance of success in the eleven-plus examination. So he goes, conscious of his failure, to a school commonly regarded as a school for failures, a school which often has both larger classes and a more limited range of courses than the grammar school. It takes an unusually gifted and/or determined child to refuse to accept these handicaps, to fight and overcome them. How many accept with resignation the mark others have put on them after only six years' schooling, cannot be fully known.

Finally, the interview, as an instrument of fine objective judgement among candidates already ranked close together, is fantastically unsound. No survey rates its validity high. Personal impressions in a short interview are much too haphazard, too liable to be influenced by chance remarks or by the child's speech, dress, and manners. This is undoubtedly the weakest part of the eleven-plus procedure. It does nothing to refine selection at the point where accuracy and refinement are most needed; and while superficially it may give an air of extra care to the business, in fact it lowers it from the plane of detached objective assessment to that of inexpert rough justice.

Disturbed by these failings, yet unwilling or feeling temporarily unable to abandon selection at eleven, some local authorities have modified the procedure in one way or another. Some have dropped intelligence tests, partly because the idea that they could distinguish inborn ability has been exploded, and partly because coaching in similar tests – much practised in some schools, not at all in others – can give the coached child an unfair advantage. Moreover, it is undesirable that these tests should figure as a regular time-consuming part of junior-school work, as has sometimes happened. On the other hand, despite their deficiencies, intelligence tests are less unreliable instruments of selection for future academic work than are tests of attainment, or interviews, and their omission makes selection less accurate.

A much criticized feature of the eleven-plus has been

the anxiety created in children by having to sit a formal examination. To avoid this, several authorities now prefer to give a series of tests at intervals in the final year. With the same end in view, the West Riding of Yorkshire has adopted in many parts of the county the 'Thorne scheme', which provisionally allots a certain number of grammar-school places to each of the junior schools of the area, according to the school's record of eleven-plus successes in the past. In any one year the junior school submits its list of children in its own estimated order of merit. Only the borderline children are then externally assessed, by means of interviews and tests in English and arithmetic. In the light of these assessments the number of grammar-school places given to each junior school is eventually settled. The scheme has the defects of its virtues. On the one hand, most children are untroubled by any formal examination. On the other hand, for those near the border-line too much depends on the accuracy of the junior school's order of merit and on the interview.

One must conclude, therefore, that none of the modifi-cations introduced in attempts to meet both popular and expert criticism of the full eleven-plus procedure has been satisfactory. Most people would say: 'If we must have selection at eleven, let it be as fair and accurate as possible.' Intelligence tests, attainment tests in English and mathe-matics, and junior school records are all necessary, if selection is not to become even less accurate than at present. The mental testers themselves hold out no hope that it will improve significantly. Is this good enough?

The result of all this immensely honest effort by educa-tional psychologists, teachers, and administrators is this: that out of every twenty children picked for the grammar school, six or seven turn out to be unsuited to that type of education, and they keep out another six or seven of the remaining eighty sent to 'modern' schools, who should have been admitted.[1] The true picture may be worse, for it is reasonable to suppose that other 'modern' school children, discouraged by rejection (as they see it), fail to respond there as they might have done had they been allowed to proceed to a grammar school. I recall the case of a boy who scored 109 and 112 in intelligence tests before he failed the eleven-plus examination, and 113 soon afterwards. He was then admitted to a grammar school by a special arrangement; and six weeks after the third test already mentioned, a now confident boy recorded a score of 134.[2] Success breeds success, and failure breeds failure.

If we are to help all children effectively, we certainly must assess their various qualities, measure and appraise them. Tests of various kinds are valuable and necessary for this purpose. Indeed, we need more guidance which is scientifically informed. But such information must be used to advance the progress of all children on a broad and varied front: the open road to personal fulfilment. Instead, we are today using it as a regulator, a turnstile through which people are allowed to pass only in single file on production of standardized credentials.

The Crowther Report found that twenty-two per cent of Army recruits to national service, and no fewer than twenty-nine per cent of R.A.F. recruits, had had the wrong type of schooling. No observer could find such figures less than gravely disturbing. Is there not, he must ask, some satisfactory alternative which could dispense altogether with selection and segregation at eleven-plus?

1. cf. Yates and Pidgeon, *Admission to Grammar Schools* (Newnes, 1957) and *15 to 18* (Crowther report), vol. I (H.M.S.O. 1959). p. 72.

2. *British Journal of Educational Psychology*, vol. XXIII, part III, November 1953, p. 151.

The comprehensive school

Between the ages of five and eleven all children, other than the educationally subnormal, the physically handicapped, and those whose parents pay fees for them at independent or direct-grant schools, attend the local primary schools (infant stage 5–7; junior stage 7–11). These primary schools are comprehensive – that is, they take practically all local children, whatever their abilities, and try to give them the education best suited to each individual pupil.

This means a common curriculum for the most part, but of course the subject-matter and the way it is presented are varied to meet the need not only of different classes but of individuals within each class. One school may prefer to have all the clever children together in one class and all the backward children in another, believing that such an arrangement will avoid frustration and facilitate the progress of both sets. Another school may hold that grading children in this way – as A, B, C, or D – damages the self-confidence of those labelled as inferior, and inhibits their future progress. The latter school will have children of widely varying ability in each class. It is therefore more likely to rely on methods which require individual teaching and learning, rather than on the more orthodox practice of teaching the whole class about the same thing and carrying the work on at the same pace for everyone.

Whichever approach is favoured, it is mainly a professional question of the best way of achieving an agreed end – the full development and progress of the individual child. Each of these primary schools is still a comprehensive school.

The comprehensive secondary school is simply an extension of the comprehensive primary school, and has the same aims. It takes practically all the children from a given district between eleven and fifteen and those who wish to stay on at school till eighteen or nineteen. Because special interests develop as people grow up, such a school must offer a wide range of courses to meet the different needs of different pupils. It may arrange the grouping of children in their classes according to age, general ability, special abilities, special interests, or a combination of some or all of these. This matter, as in the primary school, is mainly a professional one concerning the most effective way of achieving an aim about which there is no disagreement – the full development and progress of the individual pupil.

Such a school will not however be divided into distinct, separately organized sides, such as grammar, technical, and 'modern'. A secondary school so arranged would be a multilateral school, just as a school with two distinct sides (e.g. grammar/technical, technical/'modern', grammar/'modern') is a bilateral school. Multilateral and bilateral schools are uneasy compromises between the comprehensive idea and the belief that there should be distinct types of secondary school to cater for different types of child. They sometimes have the defects of both and the virtues of neither. On the other hand, several have already grown into comprehensive schools, and others are on the way.

In January 1961 there were in England and Wales 138 schools officially described as comprehensive, sixty bilateral and three multilateral schools. These numbers compare with more than 5,300 secondary schools giving a special type of education – 'modern', technical, or grammar. The comprehensives, bilaterals, and multilaterals together provided for about 186,000 children (with some 9,230 teachers); the traditional schools of separate type had some 2,500,000 children and 117,500 teachers. The proportion of children who in future will attend schools of comprehensive type, however, is rising as local authorities' plans for introducing more of them mature. The Crowther Council estimated that in 1965 over eleven per cent of secondary school children would be in comprehensive schools.

I have given the figures for schools listed as bilateral and multilateral as well as comprehensive, because official distinctions between them are by no means accurate. Two of the three schools listed as multilateral have since become fully comprehensive. Many of the bilateral schools take all local children, and some in addition are organized internally as comprehensive schools.

Another category of schools has recently appeared in the Ministry's annual statistics: 'other secondary schools' – 263 of them, with 150,000 pupils and 7,000 teachers. Some of these are essentially comprehensive. Altogether they form a fantastically mixed bag, indicating the confusion of pattern which has come upon us, and yet a vivid illustration of the Englishman's desperate refusal to take a clear-cut decision on principle and then apply it logically in practice. We must compromise: that, indeed, is itself our overriding principle.

Can we have quality with equality?

I have said that the English do not believe in equality. This is not because they are innately more snobbish or less capable of idealism than the logical French of the eighteenth century, or than the socialist Russians or democratic Americans of the twentieth. England's role in history has for so long been that of a superior nation and big brother, her people have for so long taken personal and political freedom for granted, that they are not immediately concerned with basic needs, with the upward striving of the oppressed. If 'we've never had it so good' as during the election of 1959, we have always had it pretty good compared with other countries; and so we have become less concerned with basic equality than might otherwise have been the case. With lofty superiority we have looked beyond it, searching rather for quality, and assuming that we cannot have both together.

The average Englishman is confused about the meaning and implications of equality. He takes it for granted that equality implies flat uniformity, that equality in education would impose the same subjects, the same teaching methods, the same pace of progress, on pupils who obviously differ enormously in their ability, interests, and characters.

Though some levelling-up is certainly involved, a featureless levelling-out would of course be a denial of all we have learnt from psychology and education. The differences between individuals are infinitely variable and complex; and our aim is the full development of everyone's talents.

In our consideration of the eleven-plus examination, however, we have noticed some of the difficulties met in attempting to measure these differences, to weigh, assess, *and relate them one to another* in a comparative order of overall merit. It is difficult enough to rank people in relation to one quite specific field of activity: for example, to compare two footballers, one of whom has speed and a strong shot but lacks ball control, the other slow but accurate in passing, with good ball control; or two historians, one meticulous, careful, dry-as-dust; the other imaginative, readable, and too romantic. Really accurate comparative ratings can only be made in relation to a strictly limited subject (and only then in relation to present performance, for we cannot tell how each will develop in the future) – for example, the relative speed with which six men can run 100 yards. The difficulties of judgement multiply if we broaden the field, asking less precisely 'How do they compare as runners?' (various distances being implied) or even more broadly and vaguely 'How do they compare as athletes?'

If the problems of comparative ranking are so great

within one field, whether it be athletics or art or house-craft or engineering or languages, how much more difficult is it to arrive at fair overall assessments covering still wider fields! Yet we presume to do just this with children at the tender age of eleven. For here we are in fact trying not only to assess their natural aptitudes for different subjects, but also to allow for all the complex influences of environ-ment and personality which have gone to make up the child as he is at this moment of judgement. In our present state of ignorance about the human mind and the springs of behaviour, it is insufferable arrogance not merely to predict at that early point how a person is likely to develop, but to direct him willy-nilly to one course of development rather than another.

The fact that 'modern' schools on the whole offer much poorer opportunities than grammar schools has sharpened this sense of injustice and made it obvious to all. The root failing, however, lies not in the fact that one type of school is superior to the other, but in the belief that at eleven children can and should be sorted into this type or that and educated accordingly. Improving the staff and courses of 'modern' schools will not remedy, but only tend to hide this basic flaw in our thinking about and organization of secondary education. The idea that there are two or three types of child, suitable for two or three types of school, is incredibly crude and naïve.

No two children are the same; that is a truism. The more closely we think about its implications, however, the more we realize that attempts to compare them in general orders of merit are hopelessly unscientific.

The concept of equality in education, therefore, is in fact entirely opposite to the notion of sameness and uniform-ity, of turning out all children to one pattern. It is rather the concept of equal *worth*, that is, all equally deserving and needing such aids to personal growth as we can give.

In gradually replacing birth and wealth by the ability to pass examinations, we are doing no more than replace one rule for the queueing order by another. Our philosophy is still dominated by the belief that life is a race for a few limited prizes. It is fundamentally a philosophy of limitation and restriction. Its doctrines are that the weakest must go to the wall, that the race is always to the swift and the battle to the strong. It is the bitter, cynical conclusion of the materialist.

Most of us have turned from its crudest manifestations – racial discrimination against colour and the Jews. We have half-turned against its less obvious marks – for example, the social snobberies of schooling and speech. But basically this philosophy is rooted in the idea that one can only advance at the expense of someone else, in relation to that person's failure to keep pace. It is still the law of the jungle.

Against this it is imperative that we repeat *and re-state in modern terms*, applying it in detailed argument each to our own field, the philosophy which, though to Christendom 2,000 years old, is still very new in terms of the whole span of human life on the earth. It is possible for *all* children, *all* adults, to have life and to have it abundantly; but not until we abandon our practice of appropriating the cream to a few and leaving the rest to get what nourishment they can from the blue milk.

America and Russia: a comparison

One does not need to be a selfless idealist in order to appreciate the weakness of current English thinking on education. From a materialist point of view, the deeply pessimistic belief in a limited pool of ability is causing us rapidly to fall behind in the march of progress. It is a belief rejected by the two leading civilizations of today, though they respond to this situation in different ways, neither of which is fully acceptable to the English people as a whole.

In North America – both U.S.A. and Canada – the common school is an obvious and necessary part of a democratic society. The secondary age range is from twelve to eighteen, as in Scotland. Schools vary from under a hundred pupils to several thousands in size. The former exist because they serve remote settlements as the community's only school, and inevitably offer little more than elementary education. Their number, however, is steadily declining, and they do not adequately represent the character of the normal North American high school.

Specialization in America has brought enlargement of the number of pupils, so that a school of 2,000 to 5,000 is not remarkable, with corresponding enlargement of staff, in total much more variously qualified, and enlargement of curriculum, so that different kinds of ability are all catered for.

The large American high school is no longer primarily a part of the local community, but a self-sufficient community on its own. The staff are fully absorbed in their important, ever-changing, and always demanding work. Not only are there departments staffed by specialists for all the normal subjects; there is also a guidance department run by qualified psychologists whose job it is to assess the personality and ability of each pupil and to help him to choose both the right path through school, with its multitude of options, and the right career on leaving school.

It would be wrong to suggest that these large busy schools do not look outwards. They do: but their vision necessarily ranges afar, over the whole American society in which their pupils move, and indeed beyond. As man's mobility increases, so will this trend in education. I do not believe, however, that intimate membership of a local community need obscure the wider view.

Although the Americans have more faith in specialist,

especially psychological, guidance than the English, they also have more respect for parents' wishes. Home-and-school associations flourish, and are taken for granted more than parent-teacher associations in England.

The great educational debate in North America, however, is not about the common high school, or its size, or parents' wishes, or the need for a varied curriculum, or the place of psychological guidance. It is about the grouping of children *within* the common school. At present there is little more than the occasional attempt to put the clever children in one class or stream, the average in a second, the slow in a third, and so on. This is partly because of the great influence that American parents have on what happens to their children inside the school. Segregation of a minority of the bright children would imply rejection for the majority; and few parents would willingly accept this. In general it is 'academic', often university intellectuals, who demand more selection and segregation.[1] Professional educationists on the whole resist this demand.

The American's abhorrence of imposed uniformity nevertheless permits great differences in school achievement, not only between one pupil and another, but in the study by any pupil of one subject rather than another. Within a broad curriculum, there is room for much individual choice. Rapid progress in a favourite subject can take a pupil into a class one or two grades higher for that subject, while he pursues others at a more normal pace. The result is a good deal of uneven performance: high-quality work in a few subjects, often mediocre work in the majority. Opportunity to be unequal applies not only to a whole society, but to the education of each individual.

In the Soviet Union a different social philosophy stresses

1. cf. Hilda Neatby, *So little for the mind* (Clarke and Urwin, 1953) and Jacques Barzun, *The House of Intellect* (Secker and Warburg, 1960).

the importance of equality; not only equality between different people, but the equal importance of subjects in any pupil's curriculum. There is no 'streaming': all classes are of mixed ability. The teacher will strive to take all the pupils forward together as a class in all the subjects. The work will be so organized that slow learners are helped by the quick, working in pairs or in groups. Each pupil is expected to put extra effort, not so much into his good subjects as into his weak ones.

Here, indeed, is the nub of the whole difference between the approach of the American and Soviet societies to education. The latter aims to lift the standard of knowledge and life of all its citizens. It believes that from a uniformly good standard will spring great performance and the advancement of new learning. The ground will be more fertile. Society will be well informed, educated to understand and react appropriately to the inspiration of each genius it throws up.

America, on the other hand, fears the effect of marshalling minds in standard array. It believes that the great contributions to human life have come from individuals who were allowed or were determined to assert their unique viewpoint, often flatly against the most weighty orthodox opinion. Copernicus, Martin Luther, Charles Darwin, and beyond them Jesus of Nazareth – theirs is the spirit that inspires the thought and works of America's educators, from Dewey to Conant. In short, America believes that the individual comes first, and that society is important chiefly as an environment necessary to the full life of individuals. Russia, aiming no less at achieving human happiness, regards a harmonious and efficient society as a first essential for individual fulfilment; and further assumes that individual satisfaction can best be found by serving society and subordinating one's personal desires to it.

The differences of aim are quite fine, and both have a

more than tenuous link with Christian teaching. The real differences lie in the realm not so much of philosophy as of psychology. A major issue in life is the extent to which we, individuals and societies alike, can grow to maturity. That means how far we can move from helpless dependence to easy, confident independence.

Few complete that journey. Some always retain traces of brash adolescence, the deliberate rejection of orderly living, and the assertion of individual quirks of personal likes, dislikes, and prejudices. Others live for ever under the shadow of authority. In infancy they need it. In adolescence they reject it. Where neither of these earlier stages has been completely and unhurriedly lived through, they grasp again at authority, but this time exercising it, as the easy solution. It is well known that the bullied becomes the bully. Almost every fag longs for the day when his role will be reversed. Adolescent America, authoritarian Russia, are both societies which mirror incomplete human development in different forms. Can an older, more mature social order reconcile the admirable aims of these two mutually uncomprehending young giants ? Can we in England show them, in fact, a way through the wood ?

Despite all the platitudes of politicians, too few realize how vital is education to the well-being of individuals and society. Yet its aim goes to the heart of all philosophy, to the inner purpose of all government.

I often say to parents : 'What do you want most of all for your children ?' Almost invariably they reply : 'I want them to be happy.' Happiness essentially comes with controlled but unperverted growth. It it not to be confused with soft and pleasant living. It implies, in Aristotle's sense, being usefully active, developing according to the laws of one's nature, developing the best in one's nature. Full growth demands exertion, stern testing, adaptation to the environment. Our aim as educators must be the full development of everyone's powers, schooled (because man is a social animal) for use in harmony with those of his fellows. Our pupils are like the tall young trees in the plantation, which grow up straight and strong towards the light precisely because they are in the close company of others.

We need, first, a culturally rich environment of home, school, and neighbourhood, within which children can learn and grow. We need a frank recognition that individuals are unique, their differences immensely (indeed immeasurably) varied, and demanding great flexibility of both teachers and administrators. We need to weld three outstanding features from the societies we have mentioned: the Soviet insistence on raising the educational level of all, rather than allowing a few fast starters to monopolize the field; America's concern for the freedom of the individual to move at his own best pace, along the lines he needs; England's traditional faith that only the highest standards of teaching and learning are acceptable – not merely to others, but above all to oneself. Fundamentally such a programme is a call for quality geared to the needs of a liberal, democratic society.

Can it be done? In particular, how far does the English comprehensive school succeed in its attempt to provide the answer?

2. Framework

I. EVOLUTION

WHEN, by a curious stroke of fortune, at the age of fourteen I was translated from my village elementary school to the ancient grammar school ten miles away, I entered a different world. For the first time I wore a tailored grey suit, stiff collar, and school cap. I felt a guilty turncoat when the elementary-school children of the town chanted 'Grammar, grammar matchstalks' derisively at us as we walked long-trousered through the cobbled streets.

Inside the school, too, my life was turned upside down. It was not only that for the first time I encountered such subjects as Latin and French, physics and chemistry, algebra and geometry; I had expected that. What amazed me was the elaborate apparatus devised to get boys to do what the staff wanted. Essays and tests all reaped their quota of marks, religiously added up and announced at half term and end of term. There were colours for doing well at rugger and cricket; points for one's house, prizes for this, lines or even the cane for that ... I was surprised, because none of this was known in my little village school, where we worked (and at the appropriate times played) because after all wasn't that what we went to school for? I was more than surprised, I was bewildered, because despite this host of incentives, most of the grammar-school pupils were more reluctant to do their best than any of my fellows in the village. Yet for classroom competence, devotion to their job, and interest in their pupils' progress, the grammar school staff could not have been bettered. It was the system that was different.

I had still to learn that there was yet a third world of 'public' schools operating on a level as remote from the grammar school as the latter was from the elementary school. The grammar school's strangely formal rituals were in fact copied from the 'public' school Olympians. Its best features – the teachers' deep interest in and concern for every pupil, complemented by the town's pride in its little, ancient school – sprang from the school's roots in the local community.

Up to 1944 three distinct systems of education existed in England. There were elementary, secondary, and independent schools. Local education authorities and voluntary bodies such as the churches, supported by grants from the government's Board of Education, provided free, compulsory, basic education from five to fourteen in elementary schools.

Secondary education was a superior type of education given partly in grammar schools of old foundation and partly in schools established and run by local authorities. Fees were normally charged, but some free places were given to elementary-school children who won scholarships in the examinations held around the age of eleven. The number of such free places varied widely from one district to another, but over the whole country worked out around fourteen per cent in 1944. The Labour-dominated Durham County Council ensured that every place in its secondary schools went to children who qualified in the eleven-plus scholarship examination. This 100 per cent free-place system replaced parents' wealth by pupils' ability as the criterion for admission, and anticipated the post-1944 eleven-plus examination.

Apart from the secondary schools provided or aided by local authorities, there were other schools which were either completely independent of state aid and control, or which accepted money and inspection direct from the central government ('direct grant') but not from local authorities. Many of the former were poor and far from efficient, some downright disreputable; but all gained something in the eyes of a status-seeking public from the glamour of the great independent schools. Most of these were boys' boarding schools, which were not only well endowed but whose reputation enabled them to charge high fees. Eton, Harrow, Winchester, Charterhouse, Rugby ... these and some seventy more were the schools which dominated the corridors of power. Their old pupils ran the empire, monopolized the seats in Conservative Cabinets, controlled the Foreign Office, the Treasury, the Civil Service, and the City. It was a common aim of self-made men to get their sons into such schools and ensure their future acceptance by people who mattered.

A fairly high standard of entry was demanded of candidates whose families had no longstanding connexion with such schools. Other applicants, like the young Winston Churchill many years before, found the formal examination no serious barrier. But the 'public' schools, as the most famous independent schools were confusingly called, should not be blamed for this. Their function was to educate the children of the ruling class and train them to lead. A well-known Oxford don was once heard to observe: 'Whatever the movement, good or bad, it will be led by an Etonian.' Birth and wealth still counted. The rise of the meritocracy, though imminent, had not yet begun to shape a new social order. Each 'public' school had its traditions and its special religious or educational emphasis which old pupils wanted their own children to experience. The continuity and security which the schools derived from such support was not only economic. The boarding school, being detached from the local community, needs in its place other, stable, human ties.

Nevertheless the 'public' schools were becoming anomalies in a society which, under the pressure of war, was moving rapidly towards democracy. Many of their heads and old pupils were aware of this, and in 1944 the Fleming

Report recommended that they should accept twenty-five per cent of their pupils from the State system. The recommendation has not been implemented, for it is a compromise appealing to few, and attacked by many for quite different reasons. Local authorities do not relish the prospect of losing the better pupils from their own schools and paying high fees to boot. Radical reformers dislike the idea of bolstering schools for the rich by the infusion of talent from below, and suspect that selected working-class children would be indoctrinated with upper-class attitudes. Rigid conservatives, on the other hand, fear that the special character of the 'public' school would be completely destroyed if the basis of entry were to be so largely changed.

All these points in fact are valid. The proposal has recently been revived by some of the more far-sighted heads of 'public' schools. If it comes about, it will clinch the swing-over to a meritocratic society, already far advanced in other spheres of English education.

In 1944, then, there were the three types of school: elementary for the working class, secondary for the middle class (to join which schools one working-class child in seven might aspire), 'public' or independent for the upper class. The injustice shouted aloud to a people who were, as it was the fashion for Conservative politicans to observe, 'all socialists now'; a strangely idealistic people, who in orthodox rural Skipton could choose a radical Common Wealth supporter of Richard Acland as their Member of Parliament. Such was the new force which brought into existence, with all-party approval, a great Education Act.

The 1944 Education Act

This Act made many notable decisions, not all of which have yet been implemented. The one which caught public imagination and won everyone's approval, yet whose application has aroused the most bitter controversy, was the introduction of 'secondary education for all'. In future the elementary and secondary schools were to be fused into one system, itself then re-divided into two *stages*: the first ('primary') for children up to the age of twelve, and a second ('secondary') to which all children would go – compulsorily to fifteen, and beyond that age if they wished. Eventually, at some unspecified date, the minimum leaving age was to be raised to sixteen.

It is true that independent schools were still left outside, apart from being subjected to inspection and approval by the Ministry of Education; but it was felt important not to impose uniformity. If the State schools were brought up to the best standards, it would no longer be possible for rich people to buy better material conditions by paying high fees to independent schools. The latter's justification would lie in their special characteristics – the Quaker schools' stress on religion and toleration, the Anglican atmosphere of Lancing or Marlborough, the unorthodox manliness of Abbotsholme and Gordonstoun, or A. S. Neill's revolutionary practice of love and freedom at Summerhill. It would have been a great loss to the burgeoning power of educational thought and practice had any such schools been either closed or brought under local control.

Within the State system, schools were to be maintained or aided by local education authorities, the county and county-borough councils, under the 'control and direction' of a Minister of Education. The Act said that it was the duty of these authorities to provide primary education for children up to twelve and secondary education for children aged twelve and over (later, permissively, ten years six months and over). The schools which were to provide this secondary education were to be 'sufficient in number, character, and equipment to afford for all pupils ... such variety of instruction and training as may be desirable in view of their different ages, abilities, and aptitudes, and of the different periods for which they may be expected to remain at school'.

Exception to this principle has never been taken. It is over the interpretation of the sentence that the fiercest public battle in England's educational history has been waged; and that battle is far from decided.

It might be thought that the obvious meaning was that just as a sufficient number of well-equipped primary schools is required to meet the very different needs of all the local children who go there, so each secondary school must have a full range of courses, staff, and equipment to serve the developing needs of these same children in due course, whether they stay at school beyond fifteen or not. In the same way, most independent schools take pupils with a wide range of ability and aptitude. They too need to make very varied provision for a great diversity of talent.

But the officials of the Ministry of Education, and of most of the local educational authorities, did not think in this way. Indeed, the outlook of most professional educators – teachers and administrators alike – had for a generation taken on a new slant under the influence of a school of educational psychologists whose prime concern was mental measurement.

The leading figure in this movement was Dr Cyril Burt. In 1926 he had assured the Hadow Committee that it was possible by means of intelligence tests to make a fairly accurate assessment of a child's mental capacity by the age of twelve. Burt and his followers not only thought heredity mattered far more than environment in determining mental ability, but believed they could distinguish inborn ability well enough for practical purposes. These practical purposes were the separation of clever from average children, average from dull, either in separate classes or in separate schools.

This belief in both the immediate validity and the long-term stability of intelligence testing led the Spens Committee in 1938 to recommend the establishment of three main types of school (academic, technical, and general) for children of different aptitudes and different levels of ability. The doctrine was reaffirmed in a less subtle way in the Norwood report of 1943. Its influence was clearly dominant in the White Paper which preceded the 1944 Act. The White Paper proposed that secondary education should be organized in three main types of secondary school; and though that proposal was not specifically included in the Act, the Ministry's officials were not, as we shall see, to be deterred from getting their own way in practice.

Labour Government, 1945–51

Before the issue could be brought to a head, the war-time coalition had been replaced in 1945 by a Labour government pledged to social reform. One might have supposed that an avowedly socialist party would look askance at plans for separate types of secondary school which offered courses of different length and scope to children judged superior or inferior in mental ability : schools which were, therefore, likely to vary greatly in social prestige.

But Labour was not an egalitarian party, though it included some egalitarians in its ranks. Although it had then, as now, several teacher M.P.s and the sympathy of many professors and administrators, few of the leading figures had the knowledge which would have enabled them effectively to answer the arguments of Ministry officials. Still more important, most saw no need to do so.

Much of Labour's thinking was a generation out of date. Here was a party too long starved of office, deeply concerned to make changes that were overdue. But sometimes a changed situation and new knowledge make the once-sought improvement itself inadequate. Time has overtaken it. So it was with education. Labour's general attitude here is epitomized by the attitude of the traditionally Labour Durham County Council. When secondary education had been available only to a minority, Durham had been in the van in building its own secondary schools and accepting only 'scholarship' boys and girls. Brains had rightly been preferred to wealth and birth. The bright poor boy, in the best reforming tradition, was given his chance.

The trouble was that the good party men of Durham and elsewhere were so drunk with the virtue of this advance that they failed to see it was but a step on the way. All living things change. No form of social institution can expect to do more than serve its turn usefully, before yielding place to new.

It was, then, under the nominal direction of two sincere but ill-equipped Labour ministers – first Ellen Wilkinson, then George Tomlinson – that Ministry officials took steps to ensure that their preference for a divided form of secondary education should prevail. The first of a series of Ministry pamphlets (*The Nation's Schools*, 1945) assumed that the development plans then being prepared by local authorities would be based on three types of secondary school. It offended progressive opinion, and was withdrawn; but a circular of December 1945, giving 'guidance' to local authorities on the establishment of secondary schools, proceeded on much the same assumption.

Even so, some local education authorities, notably London, Middlesex, Coventry, Oldham, and the West Riding, decided to provide comprehensive secondary schools. They were to be sufficiently large, well staffed, and equipped to meet the needs of all the pupils of the district who required full-time schooling between the ages of eleven and nineteen. The West Riding's development plan, issued in 1948, said :

The Committee ... have been unable to accept certain suggestions which have been made or implied in various reports or
Ministerial circulars. They cannot, for instance, agree that at
the age of eleven children can be classified into three recognized mental types, and should be allocated to grammar,
modern, and technical schools accordingly;

or

that the numbers to go to each type of school should be determined by an arbitrary percentage of the age group;

or

that at the age of eleven children show certain aptitudes which
can be relied upon to indicate the type of secondary school
to which a child should be alocated.[1]

But the majority of local authorities – whether from
principle, convenience, or apathy – took the other route.
The former secondary schools were re-named grammar
schools, to which only children successful in an examination at or before the age of eleven were admitted. Here and
there some authorities converted old 'junior technicals'
into technical secondary schools, to take the next layer
of ability. The senior elementary schools of pre-war
days were labelled, ungrammatically, 'secondary modern'
schools, and left to go on much as before.

The latter was much the easier course. Grammar-school
teachers were often a little fearful of being called on to
teach difficult and backward boys and girls. They had had
dull pupils before the war, it is true, but they were usually
the docile dull from respectable fee-paying families. They
disliked the possibility of losing their hitherto superior
status in the town. They thought that school standards in
scholarship and behaviour would suffer if the doors were
flung open to all. Many had little or no understanding of the
interests and needs of non-academic pupils, and felt

honestly that such pupils would be better taught by teachers who did understand them.

Conversely, the non-graduate heads and staff of the former elementary schools were apprehensive about being passed over for graduates in competition for the top jobs in a comprehensive system. Some graduates, too, realizing that their prospects of a headship in a grammar or comprehensive school were nil, chose to carve a niche for themselves in the 'secondary moderns' : better to reign in hell than serve in heaven.

But these were motives rarely voiced in public debate. The theory justifying the system was put out in 1947 in a notable Ministry of Education pamphlet, *The New Secondary Education*.

Even at the time, this pamphlet seemed remarkably naïve. Children suitable for a grammar school, dreamed the authors, 'are attracted by the abstract approach to learning'. 'Some children, on the other hand, will have decided at quite an early stage to make their careers in branches of industry or agriculture ... Others may need a course ... with a particular emphasis on commercial subjects or art. All these boys and girls will find their best outlet in the secondary technical school.' This statement, implying that a child's future path should be determined by his childish preferences at eleven, finds no support whatever in educational research. Moreover, the selection procedures devised before or since 1947 have made no serious attempt to detect special aptitudes for different kinds of job. Instead, selection is based on all-round ability. The technical school merely gets the children who fail to qualify for the grammar school, without regard to their suitability for technical education.

'The majority,' says the pamphlet, 'will do best in a school which provides a good all-round education in an atmosphere which enables them to develop freely along their own lines.' One cannot think of a better aim for the education of the minority either. Unfortunately the reality in 'secondary modern' schools was then, and still is, a grotesque distortion of this ideal. The initial stamp of failure on all incoming pupils; the large classes compared with those of selective and independent schools; an inequitable Burnham Scale which has diverted most special-responsibility payments to selective schools, with their bigger proportion of older pupils – all these have militated against the creation of an atmosphere in which very different individual needs could be met.

A lukewarm argument for comprehensive schools was presented, but it was assumed that such schools must be very large, with at least 1,500 pupils. Since nearly all secondary schools then catered for fewer than 600 children, it was clear that, if this assumption were correct, comprehensive schools must be few and far between and would have to be specially built. The case for a two-tier end-on comprehensive system, though propounded as early as 1944,[1] was not mentioned; yet it offered the one practical alternative to the tripartite system, since only by that means could all existing schools be brought economically and efficiently into a comprehensive pattern.

The hard facts which determined the attitude of the administrators were twofold. First, the theoretical pattern fitted the picture of pre-war grammar schools, junior technical schools, and senior elementary schools like a glove: it was so convenient. Secondly, the leading administrators were in general committed to segregationist practice and were reluctant to entertain the possibility that they were wrong. Widespread reform begins to gather way as they are replaced by new and uncommitted men.

Fundamentally, secondary school organization at this

1. e.g. in *The Times Educational Supplement*, 9 September 1944, R. Pedley, 'Reform in Higher Education'.

vital period (1945–51) was befogged and bedevilled by the tremendous hold on almost all educationists which the movement for intelligence testing had acquired. It would be wrong to blame Ministry and local officials too harshly for following the generally accepted evidence of the 'experts' at that time. Where comprehensive schools were planned, it was either in rural areas like the Isle of Man and Anglesey, for simple reasons of economy and efficiency, or in socialist strongholds like London and Coventry, for social-educational reasons. In general, so long as people believed that selection was being made accurately and that children's further performance could be fairly foretold by the tests in use, they were unconcerned. The destruction of the inflated claims of the intelligence testers, which was to change the whole picture, was still to come.

One highly significant feature of the political and social scene in post-war Britain, however, is spotlighted by the curious attitude of different sections of the Labour party to the question of the eleven-plus, and to the comprehensive school, throughout the period from 1944 to the present day. Whether selection could be made accurately or not, the arguments in favour of building classless yet richly diversified local communities round common schools were powerful. They were indeed an accepted part of socialist thought. Grouping by ability within these schools could still take place if desired. The alternative – forced segregation of children in separate schools, with the awful implications of daily, publicly, hammering home a child's officially assessed inferiority – should surely have been anathema to Labour. Yet, as we have seen, a Labour government, with massive electoral backing for social reform, chose the segregationist course.

London, fired by the informed vision of people like Margaret Cole and Harold Shearman, showed in its plan for comprehensive secondary education how the enormous difficulties might be overcome. A few other authorities planned likewise. But the implementation of all these plans was delayed for years by economic troubles; and in Staffordshire, Middlesex, and the West Riding, changes in political control have also meant changes in plans for secondary education before much of significance could be done.

Conservative Government since 1951

Even so, throughout the fifties there were, and in the sixties there still are, counties and county boroughs which have had undisturbed Labour majorities since 1945. Here they are:[1]

County Councils	County Borough Councils	
Derbyshire	Barnsley	Rotherham
Durham	Barrow-in-Furness	St Helens
Glamorgan	Blackburn	Salford
London	Burnley	Sheffield
Monmouthshire	Coventry	Smethwick
Nottinghamshire	Derby	Stoke-on-Trent
	Gateshead (since 1946)	Sunderland
		Swansea
	Kingston-upon-Hull	Wakefield
	Merthyr Tydfil	Warrington
	Middlesbrough	West Ham
	Norwich	Wigan

Most of these authorities have done little or nothing to apply the principles of the party to which they nominally subscribe. They plead that Conservative governments since 1951 have done all in their power to prevent or restrict a changeover to comprehensive secondary education.

That is true. If Labour has been timid, Conservative resistance has been stupidly obstructionist. In 1954, a major storm broke when the Minister of Education, Miss Florence

1. I am indebted to the Labour Party (Transport House) for this information.

Horsbrugh, refused to permit the London County Council to close Eltham Hill Girls' Grammar School and transfer these 'selected' pupils to its first big new comprehensive school, Kidbrooke. Miss Horsbrugh also refused to allow the L.C.C. to expand the Bec Boys' Grammar School into a comprehensive school.

In the following year, Miss Horsbrugh's successor, Sir David Eccles, forced the proud city of Manchester to its knees. Manchester had proposed the development of three comprehensive schools in the Wythenshawe area. Assuming that the Minister's approval would be forthcoming, it had gone ahead with its plans, and proposed to open these schools in September 1955; but the assumption was unjustified. The Minister refused to sanction two of the schools, which were new foundations, although the comprehensive development of an existing secondary school, Yew Tree, was allowed to proceed. Faced with the threatened loss of grant for the upkeep of the new schools, Manchester was forced to climb down.

Since that time, the Minister has made it clear that while he is prepared to sanction the development of comprehensive schools in rural areas and on new housing estates, he will not allow their development if it would mean the abolition of an existing efficient grammar school. Other battles have since been waged by authorities who wish to change to comprehensive schools, notably Newcastle-upon-Tyne and Newport, Monmouthshire. In Darlington and elsewhere the Minister has refused to allow the local authority to compel all children from the catchment area of a new secondary school to go there; they must be given the right to choose a grammar school place if they qualify for it.

The fact is, however, that the Minister of Education does not have unlimited powers of control. His approval is only required for the closing of an existing school, the opening

of a new one, or the enlargement of an existing school to
such a degree that it amounts in practice to a new one. If
no substantial changes in building are involved, a local education authority is free to change the character of a school
as it wishes, without consulting the Minister at all. Sir
David Eccles made this perfectly clear in the Wythenshawe
dispute when he made no attempt to restrict the comprehensive development of Yew Tree School. Lord Hailsham
and Sir Edward Boyle reiterated this principle in 1957,
when Leicestershire in effect changed some of its 'modern'
and grammar schools into junior and senior comprehensive schools respectively.[1]

Clearly, therefore, it was open to any local education
authority to tackle the real problem, the organization of
its *existing* schools, in a different way. One cannot resist
the conclusion that, although the myth of fair and accurate
selection has been exposed since the middle fifties, at least
a score of inactive Labour authorities did not want to
change. Living on the memory of past deeds and ambitions,
their character is essentially conservative. The wind of radical thought and reforming zeal chills their old bones. I began by saying that England is an aristocratic not a democratic society. It seems that a great many local Labour
Party leaders are content that this should be so.

Nevertheless, despite its patchy local record, the Labour
Party as a whole has come to a much more enlightened
position since 1951. Its policy is now clearly stated. When
it resumes office, there is little doubt that reorganization
of secondary schools on comprehensive lines will begin to
move forward.

2. THE PRESENT SCENE

During 1961–2 I obtained information on a number of

1. On the constitutional implications, cf. *Journal of Education*,
January 1958, pp. 4–5: R. Pedley, 'Lord Hailsham's Legacy'.

points from the head teachers of 120 of the 239 secondary schools in England and Wales which seem broadly comprehensive in character, and from the chief education officers of many local education authorities. The picture drawn here and in later chapters is largely based on facts assembled by personal inquiry among pupils and parents, teachers, and administrators over several years, and brought up to date in this recent check.

The rural areas

The provision of comprehensive schools in England, outside London, falls into two quite distinct categories. First in time, and in recruitment more comprehensive than anything London and the other big cities can show, come the rural areas, and especially the rural areas of the north-west.

The evolution of comprehensive education in these places owes little or nothing to educational, social, or political theories. It has been a matter of hard economics and practical efficiency. When 'secondary education for all' was decreed in 1944, most of them had only their little grammar schools, often of 100–200 pupils, to do the job. The other eleven-to-fourteen-year-olds were still in village elementary schools – indeed, the last traces of these 'all-age' schools have still not been swept away. There were no junior-technical or senior-elementary schools to tempt education committees to take the easy way out; the paper creation of new types of secondary education by writing large the old elementary forms was not possible here.

There was evidence enough in the 1940s that these small grammar schools were too small to do properly, especially at sixth form (i.e. advanced) level, even the limited job of giving an academic education to a select minority. Indeed, grammar schools of 300–500 were also inadequate in important ways. A survey which I made of twenty-one grammar schools in a midland area in 1948 showed that the average sixth form consisted of twenty-five first-year students, fourteen second-year, and four third-year. Classes of one or two pupils were common, and in forty-five per cent of the courses the first-year and second-year classes had to be taught together. Only English and French could be taken to advanced level (in those days the Higher Certificate) at every grammar school; music was not available to this standard in ten schools, biology in five, geography in three.

A national survey[1] brought out the deplorable state of affairs in the fifty-nine smallest grammar schools, each with fewer than 200 pupils:

First, second, and even third-year sixth formers have often to be taken together. 'In a small and remote school like this, sixth form work cannot be organized really efficiently,' concludes more than one head.

The basic equipment of books, laboratories, and specialist teachers – particularly in the sciences – was often sadly lacking. The situation in schools then thought of as medium-sized (200–500) was little better:

'Our sixth-form work is crippled by lack of staff and accommodation. We have only one laboratory for 250 children ... We cannot separate the first and second year sixth, or principal and subsidiary classes, and cannot offer the alternatives I would like. Six periods, for example, are given to sixth-form French, and in that class are four separate divisions among seven children.'

Clearly it was absurd to think of building small 'modern' schools parallel to the existing little grammar schools, and so multiplying inefficiency. A more sensible course was to bring all children of secondary age under one roof. More teachers, more variously qualified, could thus be available to help to educate all the children. At the same time it was

1. *The Times Educational Supplement*, 15 and 29 July 1949.

possible, at less overall expense, to build better schools, provide more and better equipment, and offer a greater range of courses to meet the different needs of a complete age-group.

The education authority of the Isle of Man (which is not a county, and has its own government and educational system), and such counties as Westmorland, the North and East Ridings, Anglesey, Merioneth, Cardigan, Montgomery, and Brecon made possible a commonsense rural organization which is now accepted without question by the Minister. But only the two islands, Man and Anglesey, each with four comprehensive secondary schools, have a complete comprehensive system.

This rural reorganization has, wherever possible, taken the form simply of enlarging in every way – numbers, range of courses, educational opportunity – an established grammar school. It may have to be re-housed in new buildings, but the school lives on, and indeed has invariably found fresh vigour. Its roots are more firm, reaching to and drawing from the whole local community. It can readily become the cultural heart of the market town and district, in a two-way flow of ideas and activities, knitting local society together.

Here is a prospect of completing the vision of Henry Morris, formerly chief education officer for Cambridge-shire, embodied in the village colleges of that county. Between the wars Morris added adult wings and adult tutors to his senior elementary schools; he used buses to bring people in to these centres from surrounding villages and hamlets in the evenings and at weekends, and he encouraged the outflow of tutors and other help to those villages. But there was one big gap in his plan: some of the best brains were withdrawn at eleven and sent to the city for a specialized grammar-school education. The American philosopher, Baker Brownell, warned his countrymen against thus bleeding the talent of small communities.[1] In the rural comprehensive school, that does not happen. Today Impington Village College has a GCE course and some 'selected' pupils. Unfortunately this seems to be only a temporary measure, and does not indicate a change of heart in the Cambridgeshire education committee.

I write of 'prospect' rather than 'achievement' as yet. Here and there, it is true, things are happening. At Wolsingham, in the northern Pennines, the local transport companies work in close harmony with the school to facilitate excursions, out-of-class activities, games programmes, and parent-teacher association meetings. At Castletown, in the Isle of Man, Castle Rushen High School acts at once as a focal point for the cultural life of the area – all the southern part of the Island – and as a fertilizing agent in the little town and surrounding villages. For example, parents and friends join in the school orchestra; children in turn are members of local bands and music societies. This interaction goes on in a number of ways. Not least important is the constant informal consultation between teachers and parents about individual children.

Only in a relatively small community, one in which all the children are known not only as individuals but as members of a family who are themselves well known, is this possible. The teachers in turn are known by children and parents not only as teachers but as men and women who may join them in the cricket or football team, at whist drives, or on any other local occasion. Mutual confidence is established; and a richer, deeper education than can ever be bred in the classroom alone is the result.

But we still have too few Castle Rushens and Wolsinghams. All too often the school closes down when the buses leave at four o'clock. Some cricket and football fields remain empty all the weekend and holidays, while young

1. *The Human Community* (Harper, New York, 1951).

men and boys struggle to play well in rough pastures. There are not enough home-and-school associations. Contact between teachers, parents, and other people of the district is frequently rare and haphazard. There is much still to be done.

I believe that rural society, apathetic though it may seem – as living things commonly are when suffering from malnutrition – needs and thirsts for new life. A bigger, more dynamic conception of the role of the rural comprehensive school would help to make it possible. The natives of Roman Britain were in the habit of dedicating their altars to 'the genius of the place'. That genius is still a powerful force, readily commanding group loyalties and communal effort.

It is significant that the enlargement of rural grammar schools into comprehensive schools, while retaining their old name, has been widely welcomed by local people. Abolition of the eleven-plus bogy is, of course, an obvious relief. But beyond that, we must realize that country society is today far less stratified than town society; if there is to be secondary education for all, enforced segregation in different types of school is an artificial instrument which makes little sense to the villager.

The life of any individual is short, but the life of such established communities is long: communal roots are deep, communal memories drift persistently through the centuries. It is well to remember that the rural comprehensive school merely puts right a modern aberration. Basically it is a reversion to the conditions of the seventeenth century, when many grammar schools were 'free' schools, and open to all the children of the district. For example at Moulton Grammar School, in Lincolnshire, the schoolmaster was not compelled to admit or teach any scholar who could not already read :

Nevertheless it is to be wished that he will not refuse any of the town of Moulton that will come to the school, but suffer them to learn what they can amongst the rest of the scholars, or by the help of some other.[1]

For Windermere Grammar School, now a very small comprehensive school for boys, the wheel has come full circle. The first deeds (1613) said that the school was to be free to local inhabitants, but not to outsiders; and the scholars were to be instructed in 'gramar, writing and reading and other good learninge and discipline meete and convenient for them . . .'[2] No minimum standard of attainment appears to have been required before a pupil was admitted. Today, the tiny schools of Windermere and Kelsick are being merged in a Lakes comprehensive school of 600 boys and girls which, while meeting modern needs, will strengthen the bonds between school and community and carry on the old traditions.

Fundamentally, then, the rural comprehensive school is sound. But it has one main weakness: its inability to provide at sixth-form level, economically and efficiently, a range of courses wide enough to meet the very different needs of all its pupils. For the country school is necessarily quite small. Figures obtained during 1961–2 from a sample of them show that on average some nineteen per cent of each age-group stay at school for a sixth year, ten per cent for a seventh year. This means, in a rural school of 600–700, about twenty-three pupils in the first year of the sixth form, twelve in the second year.

Such small numbers would not matter – they might even be an advantage – if general education up to eighteen were accepted policy in England; but it is not. Sixth-form students must specialize in two, three, or four subjects if they wish to go to college or university. The liberal

1. *Orders and Regulations governing Moulton Grammar School,* 1599.

2. *Windermere Grammar School: A History* (Westmorland Gazette, Kendal, 1936).

educationist, who wants schools to meet the greatly varying needs of individual pupils, favours neither the restriction of all to a common curriculum nor enforced early
specialization. What he must recognize is the advantage of
a school's being able to provide, especially for older pupils,
a considerable range of optional subjects: technical, commercial, practical, academic, and cultural.

In practice, the situation is this: that the rural comprehensive school offers a reasonably adequate range of
courses up to GCE ordinary level (taken at fifteen or sixteen) or to one or more of the lower-level certificates such
as those awarded by the Royal Society of Arts, the Union
of Lancashire and Cheshire Institutes, or the local authority itself. Such a curriculum normally includes the following subjects, with an opportunity to drop any given subject from fourteen to sixteen and emphasize others, but no
real specialization: English, French, German, Latin, history, geography, mathematics, biology, chemistry, physics,
art, music, housecraft (girls), and woodwork and metalwork (boys). Occasionally a school will introduce commercial subjects at the 14–16 stage, but this practice is less
common in the country than in the towns. Optional
courses in agriculture or horticulture may also be available.

At the sixth-form stage, however, it is usually a different story. Some small schools do offer a pretty full programme (I have found four schools, 350–650 in size, each
offering eighteen subjects in the sixth), but eight to fifteen
subjects is much more common, and essential subjects like
history, geography, biology, chemistry, physics, or art are
occasionally missing at this level. Yet country boys and
girls must not be denied opportunity comparable to that
of town children. The potential gap is most readily ex-
plained by listing the kind of sixth-form curriculum from
which a pupil attending a large, new, well-provided urban
comprehensive school may choose:

English; modern languages (French, German, Russian, Spanish); classics (Latin, Greek, ancient history); geography; history; economics; pure and applied mathematics; sciences (botany, zoology, chemistry, physics); art and architecture; domestic subjects (needlework, cookery, hygiene, etc.); pre-nursing courses; commercial subjects (accountancy, shorthand, typing, commercial geography and economics); engineering; technical drawing; heavy crafts (building, woodwork, metalwork); music.

I would agree that say twelve subjects judiciously chosen from the above list (e.g. English, French, German, Latin, history, geography, biology, chemistry, physics, mathematics, art, music) afford a not unreasonable choice for most members of the kind of sixth form we know in the grammar schools; but today that is not enough. Although we still have our academic pupils, they are being joined by others whose eyes are not set on universities, whose interests and needs range wider but are no less important than those of the intellectual pupil.

Even when a small school does, most nobly, extend its sixth-form curriculum to meet this challenge, it is inevitable that many classes will consist of only one or two pupils, and that some pupils at different stages of their work will have to be taught together. Classes can be too small for educational efficiency, as well as too big. At this stage the optimum size is perhaps eight to twelve: small enough for each pupil to get individual attention from the teacher, and big enough to encourage the cross-fertilization of ideas within the group – one of the most potent factors in learning.

Can we afford the extravagant use of scarce highly-qualified staff – an extravagance not matched nowadays even by the universities – which the small sixth form entails? Can the expensive items of equipment now essential for advanced studies in science and technology be used sufficiently, in this situation, to justify their provision? Will not a local education authority be very naturally inclined to economize here – and by so doing restrict the education which ought to be available to all its young people? It may, of course, be argued that it is the duty of the local authority to prime the pump, and that if extra staff, equipment, and courses were provided, more and more pupils would stay to take advantage of them.

Here is a problem which must be tackled. I believe there is a solution, which would both preserve the community school and enrich the higher secondary education of country boys and girls; and much that follows in later chapters will be devoted to its exposition.

The Isle of Man is a good example of the pros and cons of rural comprehensive schools. Douglas, the main town (25,000 population), has separate boys' and girls' secondary schools, 1,000 and 900 strong respectively. Ramsey Grammar School (now comprehensive, with some 550 boys and girls) serves the north of the island, Castle Rushen High School (450 boys and girls) the south.

Particularly good features in all four schools are the integration of school and local community and the excellent examination results. In the whole island, however, there are usually only some 100 sixth-formers distributed among the four schools. The courses available in the sixth form lack some essential subjects (e.g. history at one school), and there are several classes with only one or two pupils. From a social point of view it seems a pity to separate these comparatively few sixth-formers.

Three steps might be considered with the aim of completing a first class comprehensive system in the island: (1) the merging of the present boys' and girls' schools in Douglas, preferably in new buildings, to produce a mixed school of about 1,600 pupils aged from eleven to sixteen; (2) the limiting of Ramsey and Castle Rushen, likewise, to an eleven-to-sixteen range, with 400–500 pupils in each; (3) the establishment in Douglas of a sixth-form college for the whole of the island, with a boarding house to accommodate during the week those pupils from a distance; they could, if they wished, go home at week-ends, as happens now in the Soviet Union. The establishment of a small comprehensive school (from eleven to sixteen) in the ancient western port of Peel might also be considered.

Anglesey also has four comprehensive schools, all co-educational. Holyhead, with 1,250 children, is the biggest, with 1,000 at Llangefni, and over 800 each at Beaumaris and Amlwch. Holyhead, where a grammar school and 'modern' school were combined to produce Anglesey's first comprehensive foundation in 1949, has since set the pace, though handicapped by old and unsatisfactory buildings. Mr Trevor Lovett, headmaster of Holyhead, is the apostle of the doctrine of 'progressive differentiation' as children move up through the school year by year, a doctrine now very largely accepted throughout the comprehensive schools of England and Wales.

The Anglesey schools give a rich, full, social and cultural education. Three of Holyhead's strong suits, for example, are the sailing club, whose members have made their own sailing dinghies, Welsh and English drama, and choral work and orchestra. (More than forty pupils are receiving instruction in musical instruments; the senior school orchestra comprises two first violins, six second violins, two violas, two cellos, three flutes, two oboes, two clarinets, two cornets, one French Horn, one trombone.)

Few rural grammar schools could rival the range and quality of Holyhead's present programme. Indeed the little pre-1949 Holyhead grammar school, under the same headmaster, could not approach it. Since it became comprehensive, a stream of first-class examination results has flowed from this school. In 1959–60, for example, twelve sixth-form pupils won county scholarships, two won special scholarships, two won State scholarships, and one gained one of the nine Foundation Scholarships at King's College, Cambridge.

Anglesey's education committee at first intended that each of its comprehensive schools should specialize in certain sixth-form studies, and that pupils should transfer elsewhere if their own school could not provide what they needed. It was found, however, that boys and girls are reluctant to join another established community so late, and that head teachers do not want to lose them. It is feared that specialist teachers would be less readily attracted to a school not offering sixth-form work in a given subject. Some boys and girls, moreover, would be involved in inconvenient travel right across the island. A central sixth-form college would dispose of the first and last objections, but not the other two.

Extensive comprehensive developments in rural Wales beyond Anglesey are too little known. The percentages of thirteen-year-old pupils in comprehensive schools in the leading counties are as follows: Merioneth 66, Cardigan 66, Montgomery 55, Brecon 46, Caernarvon 32, and Pembroke 21.

Five of *Caernarvonshire*'s ten districts are served by comprehensive schools. In the other five there are grammar and 'modern' schools, and here Caernarvon now uses the West Riding's 'Thorne scheme' of selection in place of the old eleven-plus examination.

Flintshire is distinguished by having two Welsh-speaking bilateral schools, one for the east and one for the west of the county. All staff and pupils are bilingual, and official functions such as assemblies, concerts, and governors' meetings are in Welsh.

Four of the five secondary education districts in *Merioneth* are served by small comprehensive schools of

400–600 pupils, and the fifth will shortly come into line. *Montgomeryshire*'s secondary education, too, is almost entirely comprehensive, in the sense that in six of the seven districts all children go to their local high school, and the eleven-plus examination has been abolished there. The exception is Welshpool, where the grammar and 'modern' schools are being brought close together, with a joint assembly hall for two new buildings. In the fullness of time, integration will doubtless result.

Cardigan has four comprehensive schools, at least one of which has developed a technical stream. This school also has a further-education department, with 150 day-release classes studying for the Ordinary National Certificate and the London City and Guilds examinations: a small but practical taste of what might be done to link the full-time and part-time education of adolescents and avoid the cultural split which otherwise may yet follow comprehensive schooling.

Pembroke has four comprehensive schools, and *Breconshire*'s pattern is similar. Its comprehensive school at Ystradgynlais, 850 strong, has made it possible to abolish the eleven-plus in the surrounding district. In other counties comprehensive schools are fewer, or non-existent; but here and there new proposals are being discussed, including possible experiments with junior and senior high schools.

Rural Wales, then, has already gone most of the way towards a complete pattern of comprehensive secondary schools. In some respects the framework has marched ahead of internal school organization. Most schools still provide separate 'grammar' and 'modern' courses, and children are still thought and spoken of as belonging to one of these 'types'. In most – there are two or three exceptions – the range of sixth-form courses is too limited, and technical education is particularly deficient. The size of each sixth-form class is usually well below the optimum standards which combine economy of staff with efficiency in teaching and learning.

Nevertheless, as I shall show later in this book, examination results surpass those of similar areas which are organized on a segregated basis. Wales has no reason to be dissatisfied with the educational example she has set to England in this as in so many other matters.

Progress in rural England has lagged far behind that in the Principality. *Westmorland* has Windermere, Kirkby Stephen, and Appleby. The inspiration at Windermere was provided by a liberal chairman of governors, but the evolution of Kirkby Stephen (formerly a tiny girls' grammar school) and Appleby (formerly a tiny boys' grammar school) owes more to practical considerations than to high-minded educational philosophy.

This explanation also applies to the *North Riding*, which believes in selecting only one pupil in six for separate grammar schools, where the population is big enough to justify them. However, it has established three secondary schools, each of which takes all the local children, in sparsely populated districts. Perhaps, when it comes to consider possible extensions of the comprehensive principle, the North Riding County Council will heed the words of its revered Lord Lieutenant, Sir William Worsley. On his first visit to the new school at Thirsk, Sir William said:

There is nothing new about comprehensive schools. It is the oldest form of education in the world. Nearly all our great public schools began as grammar schools, as you did, and then spread their wings and took in more and more subjects until they became comprehensive schools. That system has worked wonderfully and has been copied all over the world.[1]

There are other rural comprehensive or near-comprehensive schools, whose size ranges between 300 and 1,150,

1. *Darlington and Stockton Times*, 26 July 1958.

here and there in the north. The main drive here, however, comes from the *West Riding*. This county has long been inspired by two major figures in the movement towards comprehensive education, Alderman W. M. Hyman and Mr A. B. Clegg. For many years Mr Hyman has dominated the scene of West Riding local government. His forceful attacks on eleven-plus segregation have been supplemented by the particular interest of the chief education officer, Mr Clegg, in new ideas. As a result, the West Riding is today a seed-bed of experiment.

It has nine full comprehensive schools, opened between 1950 and 1962. More are to be built in the next few years at various centres, and amalgamations of existing 'modern' schools, or 'modern' and grammar schools, are also taking place. A system of junior and senior high schools at Hemsworth, with transfer of all pupils at fourteen, has been approved in principle by the county, and similar schemes are envisaged for Castleford and part of the Don Valley, though all await major building projects. At Mexborough an important innovation is a junior college attached to the grammar school, which is to house both the grammar-school sixth form and all pupils from 'secondary modern' schools in the area who wish to continue their education. The 'Thorne scheme', already referred to, has spread to many of the areas where eleven-plus selection must for the present, at least, remain.

The northern pattern has now been with us for some years, and the occasional new rural school there causes no surprise. The midlands, too, are familiar with comprehensive schools of various kinds. *Oxfordshire*, for example, has two and is to have two more, at Kidlington and Bicester.

More significant is the recent appearance of quite large comprehensive schools, well-organized and having no nonsense about grammar/'modern' bilateralism, in the conservative south-west. *Dorset* has two of them: Colfox

School at Bridport, the first rural comprehensive in the West country, opened in 1956; and Gillingham, opened in 1959. Two more will open in 1963, at Lyme Regis and Beaminster. Colfox, with 930 girls and boys, is already keeping half of each age-group for a full fifth year and twenty per cent for a sixth year. In 1959 *Devon* opened a comprehensive school at Tavistock, and plans another for Ilfracombe. A formerly bilateral school at Plymstock has now become comprehensive. *Cornwall* has started a bilateral school at Camelford, absorbing an old grammar school of 200 boys and girls, and seems likely to adopt a junior/senior high-school pattern at Saltash. In the south-east, *Kent* is to enter the lists with a new comprehensive school. In addition the counties of Gloucester, Hereford, and West Suffolk each have one or more bilateral schools whose 'grammar' and 'modern' sides are usually growing closer together.

Two recent setbacks to this rural spread must be recorded: the decision of Kesteven (Lincolnshire) to discontinue the bilateral character of the Robert Pattinson school, and the abandonment of a longstanding plan for a bilateral school at Eye, in Suffolk, which may now lose its little grammar school altogether. These apart, the picture in the countryside of England and Wales is one of quiet, steady, comprehensive growth. It is unobtrusive, but to a countryman no less impressive or exciting for that. The director of education for Anglesey in 1962 made a comment which sums up the rural attitude: 'I do not think that I have once, since I assumed my present post about two years ago, heard any member of the Education Committee express regret that the present policy came to be adopted.'[1] Yet, apart from the West Riding and Derbyshire, this rural development owes little or nothing to political or educational doctrine. It is a matter of hard sense, of economy and efficiency.

1. *Education*, 23 February 1962.

So the rural scene is being steadily filled up along these lines. The grammar schools, along with their poor relations the 'modern' schools, who in the nature of things must always be with them, are gradually withdrawing to prepared positions, immensely strong positions, in the towns and cities. There we must follow them; for England is now a nation of town dwellers, and it is to the towns that we must turn for the clash of ideologies and the first skirmishes of battle.

The towns: new centres of population

Outside the rural areas; the impulse towards comprehensive schooling has been very different in origin and has followed a much more stormy course. The enlargement of the country grammar school was seen to be the logical, sensible way of providing for rural communities which were little concerned about the refinements of social status. The problem in the towns, where large, efficient, selective schools (grammar and sometimes technical too) were entrenched, was much greater.

The grammar schools' great prestige gave them a powerful and pervasive voice in national affairs. Their old scholars, inevitably, often held responsible positions in local government, the local Press, industry, and commerce. Old boys and old girls, former teachers and headmasters, were all filled with a nostalgic affection for *alma mater* who had helped to make them what they were. As parents in a status-conscious society, they were naturally anxious that their children in turn should have at least the 'advantages' which they had themselves enjoyed; and they were joined in this desire by those worthy working-class parents who hoped to see *their* children move out of the pit or the factory and get a white-collar job. Almost all these people favoured selection for grammar schools – provided their children were among the selected.

Here, however, was the first chink in the defences of the existing order. As the years went by, the number of disappointed and vocal parents inevitably grew. On the sidelines stood many influential products of the independent schools, which had never paid much regard to selection by ability anyway. Quite a lot of them were sympathetic to the comprehensive idea. At first they watched as though it were a street fight which did not really concern them; but one or two of the bolder spirits have begun, very recently, to declare themselves on the side of the reformers. The cutting edge of the attack on eleven plus and the segregated system, however, came from the professional educationists like Simon, Floud, and Daniels, who dissected its weaknesses and held up its fallibility for all to see. They established a position of strength from which reform must come.

Repeatedly, however, England has preferred evolution to revolution. Our rulers' most masterly tactics, over the centuries, have been the ordered retreat, the skilful, gradual, unnoticed shifting of position, the absorption of the ideas of the reformers, and ultimately – suitably modified and maybe under a new guise – their adoption.

This is what is happening in English secondary education today. In view of mounting popular pressure and the growing weight of expert evidence, it would have been suicidal for a Government to ban comprehensive schools altogether. Indeed, I am sure that the process of strategic withdrawal, of cushioning and absorbing the attack, is largely an unconscious one. There is today a more tolerant climate at the Ministry, a sincere open-minded approach well expressed by its Senior Chief Inspector of Schools, Mr Percy Wilson:

This [the organization of secondary education] is a matter where most of us have been emotionally involved and I think we are most of us guilty, in the past, of having said some foolishly dogmatic things. I know I have. We have taken sides on *a priori* grounds, in ignorance or partial ignorance of the real criteria of judgement. ... There is room for co-existence. I would go further – there is *need* for co-existence.[1]

So we have a policy which is really the policy of Sir David Eccles, laid down during his first period of office. This is: to accept the case for rural comprehensive schools, and to allow new comprehensives to be provided, where the local authority wishes it, in new centres of population such as the new towns and housing estates; but to draw the line at changing the character of established grammar schools in towns and cities by enlarging or absorbing them into comprehensive schools.

For the present, the cards are stacked against the comprehensive school. The grammar schools have been given breathing-space to remedy some weaknesses, to broaden their courses so that more and more are becoming grammar/technical, and to take advantage of the national trend towards longer voluntary schooling by building up their sixth forms and forcing wider the doors to Oxford and Cambridge. The result is, to quote Mr Wilson again, that 'the grammar schools have proved both tough and adaptable, and they are probably in a stronger position today than before the first comprehensive school was built.'

I have remarked on the apprehensive attitude of many local Labour parties to the reorganization of their secondary schools on comprehensive lines. The Ministry's go-slow policy may come as a relief to those who are not anxious to take more serious action. It enables honour to be satisfied, feelings of guilt assuaged. An 'experiment' is being carried out: enough! For the rest, let sleeping dogs lie. The electoral consequence of plumping for wholesale reorganization of a city's secondary education, it is feared, might be disastrous.

1. *Views and Prospects from Curzon Street*, 1961, pp. 16–17.

The Ministry's policy entails a further handicap for comprehensive schools. It is well known that the cultural background of most of the people who move from city slums to new council housing estates is distinctly poorer than that of a cross-section of the nation. When the Minister insists, as he does, that children within a comprehensive school's catchment area have the right to try for a grammar-school place, and to accept it if they are successful, the loss of these few is a grievous blow to the local school. It may fill their places with children of nearly comparable ability from outside the normal catchment area who have just missed a grammar school place, or whose parents prefer them to attend a comprehensive school. But this does not compensate for the effect on the school's local prestige when the brightest children go elsewhere.

West Bromwich produced an ingenious and very fair solution to this problem. They asked the parents of all children in the last year of the junior schools at Churchfields (the comprehensive school district) whether they favoured comprehensive education or selection for a particular type of school (grammar/technical/'modern') according to the diagnosis of the eleven-plus examination. If they preferred the former, the child did not sit the eleven-plus but went direct to Churchfields. If the latter, he took the eleven-plus and was allocated according to one of the three separate types; but if he failed to get into a grammar school, he could not change his mind and take the comprehensive school as second best. In fact over ninety per cent of the parents chose the comprehensive school and no eleven-plus. In 1961, however, Labour lost control at the municipal elections, and the new council modified the system, enabling children who take the eleven-plus to fall back on Churchfields as a second choice.

All the urban comprehensives suffer to a greater or less

extent in this way from creaming by the grammar schools. The effect on the more difficult areas, housing estates resulting from slum clearance, is best shown by an example, which shall be nameless.

The rapidly expanding population of this estate has, of course, no local roots and is often restless and destructive. The health of many families on the estate is below average, and school attendance is difficult to enforce. The juvenile court is all too familiar to many children. The average ability is low, as the following figures from one comprehensive school on the estate show:

Year of entry:	1959	1960	1961	1962
Intelligence Quotient (national average 100)	86	91	88	92
English Quotient (national average 100)	82	94	91	95
Arithmetic Quotient (national average 100)	87	91	94	96

An annual intake of at least two forms (sixty pupils) and preferably three forms (ninety pupils) of normal grammar-school ability is usually thought desirable for the proper organization of GCE courses. In this school the figures are:

Year of entry:	1959	1960	1961	1962
Number of pupils of grammar-school ability (i.e. local 11 + successes)	8 (2.5%)[1]	8 (1.8%)	20 (4.3%)	7 (1.4%)
Borderline	9 (2.8%)	7 (1.6%)	11 (2.3%)	10 (2.0%)
	17	15	31	17

It is a silent tribute to the quality of the staff and their leader that in these days when too many 'vote with their

1. Figures in brackets show the percentage of the total age group.

feet' at the first sign of difficulty, only one teacher from a staff of thirty-six left the school during the year before this was written. These undervalued teachers are the men and women who, while other people put on their slippers and relax before the telly, organize school clubs from seven to nine p.m. Their holidays frequently take the form of youth-hostelling with their boys and girls, or the strenuous, responsible business of organizing and supervising school visits both in England and abroad.

One of the rural comprehensive schools' biggest advantages is denied to almost all their urban counterparts. The rural school carries the grammar-school cachet, the name and something of the mellowness of a school with tradition. Its new aspect is but the latest stage in a long period of growth. How different the task of the school which springs from the little-regarded 'secondary modern'! Even more tough is the job of welding two 'modern' schools and their staffs into a whole, giving it unity of purpose and social harmony. The new school starting completely from scratch is in a neutral position; the slate is clean, however, and most heads would prefer to begin like that.

It would be wrong to be pessimistic, in spite of the very real difficulties. One school, in a rural setting beyond the Black Country, began as a 'modern' school in 1951 and immediately started a GCE course. In 1961 pupils from the 1954 intake were going to university and training college. It is now the social and intellectual centre of the estate. Its Community Association, of which the headmaster is the Warden, has raised over £1,000 for the library; five complete ballets have been produced in the past ten years, of a standard comparable to professional productions; and there are regular exchanges with pupils from France, Germany, and Sweden.

Progress is being made, but it is an uphill fight. One thing is sure. If, from adversity, the comprehensive schools can rival or surpass national achievements under the segregated system, both in such things as examination results, and in the qualities which are more slowly assessed by public opinion such as good conduct, cooperation, keenness, and acceptance of only the highest standards, the case for complete reorganization of our secondary schools will be irresistible. Our comprehensive schools are still all pioneers. The burden of proof rests with them.

Let us look at the most important features of some of these urban centres. The situation in *Coventry* is, in simpler form, the nearest in the provinces to that in London. This bomb-shattered city, now rebuilt in imaginative style, and the heart of Britain's motor industry, looks back with pride on its ancient past; but it also looks forward to the future. Culturally it sets the pace for the Midlands, with its cathedral, its central precinct, and its theatres. It is to have a new university, and, as one would expect from such a progressive authority, its secondary school system has been a model for developments elsewhere.

Coventry today has eight comprehensive schools, each some 1,200–1,600 in size. Eventually it may have fourteen. Each is organized on a House basis; that is, in addition to administrative and teaching quarters, there are detached blocks on the campus which serve as the social centres for smaller groups of children. They are intended to be the day school's equivalent of the residential Houses at boarding schools. The Houses are built in pairs, with a central kitchen and dining hall, and accommodation for one House in each wing: general-purpose rooms (which have unfortunately to be used as classrooms), prefects' room, small staff-room, housemaster's or housemistress's room, and cloakrooms. Foxford School prefers to have four Houses of 350 children each occupying a complete block, rather than eight houses of 175 children each in a semi-detached wing and sharing some essential services. Five pairs – ten Houses of 150 children each – is the aim as Coventry's normal pattern.

This decision to give physical embodiment to a House organization is Coventry's special contribution to the evolution of the comprehensive school in England. It has been adopted at neighbouring West Bromwich too, and the pattern will undoubtedly spread.

Most of Coventry's comprehensive schools are in beautiful surroundings near the fringe of the city, with spacious playing fields, lawns, and flowering borders. Caludon Castle School occupies over sixty acres spanning the valley of the River Sowe. Woodlands School stands in fifty-two acres of a former nature reserve. Some day, it is hoped, each neighbourhood will have its own comprehensive school to which all local children will go.

At present this is not possible. There are still a score of 'modern' schools which must be used, and four grammar schools, two of which are boys' direct-grant schools and two girls' maintained schools. These four schools, with their longer tradition and record of academic success, naturally attract the ablest children, and this in turn helps them to maintain their lead. The comprehensive schools may fill their places with other eleven-plus successes – though of a lower academic calibre, as judged at that stage – from other neighbourhoods which do not yet have their own comprehensive school; but as new schools are built, bright children are spread more thinly among them, and the prospect of really good sixth-form work dims. Moreover, the arrangement leads to comprehensive schools being ranked in public esteem as second-best. In the circumstances, one wonders whether West Bromwich's former policy could not be adopted here and in other areas similarly placed.

Bristol is the only city other than Coventry whose circumstances closely resemble those of London. In all three,

Labour-controlled councils have been inspired by ideals of social and educational equality. All three have built their new, handsome, well-equipped secondary schools on comprehensive lines. In all three the existence of independent and grammar schools, which for one reason or another cannot be absorbed, has meant that the comprehensive schools receive few children of very high intelligence, and these are mainly late developers whose quality the eleven-plus examination cannot detect.

When the new schools, rather smaller than Coventry's, were first opened in Bristol in the mid fifties, the whole idea was unpopular with the general public. There are now seventeen such schools, comprehensive in spirit if not in name, and as one head says, 'increasing numbers of good academic pupils are opting for these schools in preference to the traditional grammar schools'. Labour has now lost control of Bristol, but all the comprehensive schools envisaged in the development plan have now been provided, so little further change was in any case likely.

Outside London, Coventry, and Bristol the appearance of urban comprehensive schools has been scattered and piecemeal. *Birmingham* has two large schools in the 2,000 category and will soon open a third. The main feature distinguishing them from schools of similar size in London or Coventry is their organization in lower (eleven to thirteen), middle (thirteen to fifteen), and upper (fifteen to eighteen) schools, in separate but closely adjacent buildings. There is one head, but he has deputies in charge of the lower and middle schools described as 'head of the lower/middle school'. This pattern at first owed its existence to the Ministry's preference for three blocks, in case reversion to three types of school should be thought necessary, but has proved to have considerable advantages.

Staffordshire has provided four comprehensive schools on the Black Country fringe, and two more are envisaged.

They were originally meant to admit no more than 150 children a year and to have a total of 750–800 when fully developed. In order to provide among them a wide range of sixth-form courses, each school was to specialize in the rarer subjects, and it was hoped that pupils would move across to another school if necessary. Such cross-transfers are not popular with either staff or pupils, as Anglesey has found. However, pressure of numbers has in fact compelled the Staffordshire schools to take more than 200 children each year, and to top the 1000 mark. It seems unlikely that any sixth-form traffic among the different schools will ever materialize.

Developments in three very different areas merit a special note. Their circumstances are poles apart. In the new town of *Crawley*, the Thomas Bennett School was opened as a bilateral school in 1958. In practice it is already comprehensive. It has rapidly won public esteem by reason of its scholastic work, the vigour of its societies, and the conduct and deportment of its pupils. It aims at really high academic standards. With an uncreamed intake – unique phenomenon in a town – it has taken over sixty pupils a year on a four-year course to GCE ordinary level in six subjects. The first group passed in seventy-two per cent of all the subjects taken – which included Russian – and some fifty have started a three-year sixth-form course.

Ashlyns School, at Berkhamsted in *Hertfordshire*, also is making its mark, with close on fifty per cent of its pupils gaining at least one pass at the ordinary level of GCE and twelve to fifteen per cent eventually gaining at least five passes. Already five of its pupils who failed the eleven-plus have entered universities.

The future progress of these two schools is of special significance for the comprehensive movement in England. We are an urban people. Further, the centre of national life, of cultural and political activity and decision, has shifted and is still shifting from north to south. It is in areas like Sussex and Hertfordshire, especially, that the professional classes swarm; and it is their opinion which will ultimately decide the issue betwen segregated and comprehensive education. Though – competing for higher status in a competitive society – they are conditioned in favour of the former, they are nevertheless trained to look at facts and to reason from them. If Thomas Bennett and Ashlyns produce the goods in the heart of conservative territory, a revolution in thinking will soon be under way.

The situation on the *Kirkby Estate*, an overspill area for Liverpool, in some ways contrasts markedly with that at well-to-do Crawley. Kirkby is not only a working-class area, but very largely a slum-clearance area. There is indeed something like a common culture here, but it is far from comprehensive. Socially it is a one-class new town. There has been little time for adjustment, for shaking down. The Kirkby of 1952 was a village of 1,200 people, with 134 schoolchildren. Ten years later it was a town of over 52,000 with 16,600 schoolchildren. In 1952 there were five teachers, in 1962 there were 648.

There are four comprehensive secondary schools: two county mixed (Brookfield and Ruffwood), and two Roman Catholic (St Gregory's for girls and St Kevin's for boys). Each of the four will ultimately have a yearly intake of 360 pupils, and an expected total size of perhaps 1,750 pupils. Ruffwood and St Kevin's, planned from the start as comprehensive schools, have separate House blocks. Brookfield and St Gregory's, using separate buildings originally intended for 'modern' schools, are developing a lower and upper school organization not unlike that at Birmingham.

Fundamentally, Kirkby's problem is lack of roots and social stability. At first the schools were in flux, because new children were constantly drifting in: at the end of its first year Brookfield was fifty per cent larger than when the year began. The growth of the town is now, however, largely complete. The need not only for a community centre, but for leadership from such a centre, is very great – and it must serve families as well as individuals, adults and teen-age workers as well as children.

Here is a stern challenge to the staffs of comprehensive schools whose interest reaches beyond merely teaching children with a wide range of ability; and the teachers at Kirkby have bravely picked up the gauntlet carelessly tossed down by an affluent society. They are giving the people of this one-class town what they need more than anything else: hope, self-respect, the real prospect of a long, hard, rewarding climb to a satisfying individual and communal life. Good keen teachers with a sense of vocation are more easily recruited to a comprehensive than to a 'modern' school in this kind of situation.

Children and parents realize that the doors of opportunity are open to the deserving. Already Brookfield School holds seventy per cent of its pupils for a full fourth-year and one third of them for a full fifth-year course. It is in such situations, if anywhere, that attention to such insignia as school uniform can be justified, for they help to promote the prestige of the school and the personal standards of living of its pupils. At Ruffwood, for example, over ninety per cent of the children wear school uniform. The great majority, proud of their school and its equipment, use both well.

At present children who pass the eleven-plus examination may choose to go to grammar schools outside the area. For years to come, a combination of working-class outlook and below-average academic talent seems likely to hinder the development of really good sixth-form work in each individual school. Will the local and Roman Catholic authorities consider providing a sixth-form college, or better still a 'county college' for both full-time and part-time education, to serve the whole Kirkby community? Here would be a splendid setting for a great experiment un-encumbered by deep-rooted vested interest. On the other hand it is fair to say that advanced work is already develop-ing. Brookfield, for example, now has a sixth form of more than forty pupils, many of whom are studying for the advanced level of GCE.

Meanwhile the schools are helping to weld the new com-munity, enriching the life of all, not only children and their parents. There are normal contacts with the welfare services, industry, the churches, and so on. Children and teachers play their part outside school: thus the children help to run a junior Road Safety Council. Other people come in: a section of the Liverpool Philharmonic Orchestra, for example, and speakers on different subjects. While the Thomas Bennett School thrives at Crawley, the Kirkby comprehensive schools, no less worthily, are showing what can be built under more adverse circumstances. As the headmaster of Brookfield says: 'The school itself is a community, but not a closed one, helping to form the new urban community of today and tomorrow.'[1]

London

It was Hitler and Göring, with all their evil apparatus of war, who made possible London's educational 'new look'. Not only did they damage or destroy 1,150 out of the 1,200 schools and departments, but they provoked in the people of the capital a reforming zeal, a vision of a better world, which in this century has been one of the curious compensations thrown up by savage destruction. Decades of slothful peace do not, alas, achieve so much.

The practical expression of this idealism came in the

1. *Forum*, 11, 2, p. 58.

County of London Plan – a great sociological document which foreshadowed a proud and busy future for each of London's neighbourhoods and boroughs, knit harmoniously in a cooperative whole. The London School Plan, adopted by the County Council in March 1947 and approved by the Minister of Education in February 1950, was a necessary complement to the larger scheme. In particular, the decision to rebuild secondary education on the basis of comprehensive schools was a powerful reinforcement to the idea of neighbourhood communities.

During 1946–9 eight experimental comprehensive schools were established. Their buildings were old and sometimes separated by more than one street, for new secondary-school building was not then permitted. All the pupils had fallen at the great eleven-plus hurdle, education's Becher's Brook. Working in depressing material conditions, both teachers and pupils needed limitless faith and encouragement. Parents, too, had to be convinced that the new aims were worth while; and this was made no easier by the stream of lordly condemnation which poured from eminent but ill-informed lips and was given prominence in the national press.

It was in these circumstances that the calibre of the eight chosen head teachers was tested and vindicated. They were the pioneers who hewed a path through the jungle of obscurantism and cultural poverty. I recall most vividly – no other word is appropriate – Miss O'Reilly of Walworth. The Irish are at their best when fighting against odds, whether in Connemara or the Congo. Here was one of the first women heads of mixed schools, the flame of whose idealism, energy, and love fired many of those children, and their teachers and parents, with faith in themselves and in their school. There were others too, who in their different ways paved the way for the handsome, assured Mayfields and Tulse Hills of the future.

It was at these 'interim comprehensives' that individual children began, most startlingly, to shatter general belief in the validity of eleven-plus selection and the relative permanence of the 'intelligence quotient' (I.Q.). 'Jean Smith', for example, started in the lowest stream of the lowest class with an I.Q. of 96, languished for three years, and then came to life; she passed in seven subjects at GCE ordinary level, including Latin in one year, and went on to become a teacher. 'David Jones', another teacher, came in his fourth year from a local 'modern' school with an I.Q. of 80; two years later he passed in five subjects at GCE ordinary level and went on to study English, history, scripture, and music.

Such examples of late development are now almost commonplace. They have always occurred in independent schools, but little notice has been given to examples from this field.[1] It was the earliest comprehensive schools, in London and elsewhere, which furnished much of the ammunition which has shot to shreds the intellectual case for a stratified pattern of education, taken for granted less than twenty years ago.

When London took up the post-war threads, there were four main types of secondary school ripe for re-organization apart from the independent and voluntary grammar schools. They were county grammar schools, 'central' schools for borderline eleven-plus cases, junior technical schools still mostly housed in technical college buildings, and the former senior elementary schools, which

1. cf., however, O. M. Slaney, *I.Q. and O Level* (*The Times Educational Supplement* 25 September 1959), who showed that 93% of boys at Lancing College with I.Q.s under 115 gained 'good' GCEs; and L. Bruce Lockhart, letter in *T.E.S.*, 22 September 1961: 'One of the Gresham's pupils who failed at 11+ and 12+, after a full range of O levels got distinction in two A levels plus an alpha in the general paper – a case which is, I am sure, typical of most good public schools.'

took the unfortunate children who had failed to qualify for any of the above types of school. This pattern was gradually changed. Some technical schools have been merged, with much better facilities, in new comprehensive schools. All the larger secondary schools, whether in old or new buildings, now provide courses of some kind beyond the fourth year.

Other problems were raised by the needs of the churches. Both the Church of England and the Roman Catholics wanted smaller secondary schools than those contemplated by the county, and both wanted some separate grammar schools. Time has modified the opinion of both churches on the question of size. The Church of England has revised its proposals in order to secure fewer but larger secondary schools than those agreed in the original plan. The Roman Catholics are likely to get both larger schools and a twenty per cent increase over the number of places originally given them.

London's main headache, however, has been the voluntary grammar schools, over fifty of them, which could not be disturbed. These schools, whose good academic records and high social prestige naturally attract parents, have continued to tap the full flow of talent which would otherwise have gone to the local comprehensive school. As in Coventry and Bristol, this is a most serious issue. The faith of all but the most ardent socialists has been severely tested when the choice has been local comprehensive school or grammar/'public' school for their own children.

In the neighbourhoods served by voluntary grammar schools, the best the London County Council could do was to provide other secondary schools, each complementary to a voluntary school in educational provision. Naturally these 'county complements' tend to be much smaller (perhaps 750–800) than the schools intended to be fully comprehensive. The latter are commonly planned to take 2,000–2,200, but their numbers are likely to be cut to 1,500–1,900 as London's population moves out beyond its boundaries. The 1947 estimate of the number of children aged eleven-plus is to be reduced by 18.6 per cent.

The county-complement system is a makeshift business, which in effect accepts the division of secondary education in these districts into 'grammar' and 'sub-comprehensive'. The council has not yet seriously considered the obvious alternative – to put these schools end-on, as in North America or Leicestershire, as junior and senior high schools. Hitherto, indeed, the grammar schools themselves would not have accepted this solution. But opinion in the country is gradually changing; and the overtures for such an arrangement may yet come from the voluntary schools rather than from the council.

The innumerable obstacles which have hindered the development of the County of London Plan have also made it extremely difficult for London to pursue effectively the aim of serving each neighbourhood with a comprehensive school. It is perhaps inevitable, but none the less disappointing, to find that London's only definition of 'fully comprehensive' is 'the intention to provide fully and equally for the needs of pupils of all levels of ability'.[1] It means that these schools do not necessarily have a true cross-section of an age-group. More important, it means that a school's catchment area is not a clearly-defined neighbourhood unit. Eltham Green, for example, is a school set up half-way between two townships, but belonging to neither.

In such circumstances a school is forced into a more self-sufficient existence than perhaps the staff themselves would desire. Vigorous school societies abound, and so do parent-teacher associations, but apart from certain schools like Haverstock, Collingwood, Walworth, and Peckham,

1. *London Comprehensive Schools*, p. 13.

which stress social service, activity is school-centred; the two-way flow, often involving people other than parents, which marks the real neighbourhood community, is missing. So the school becomes a cultural oasis in the suburban desert. Given the desert, it is invaluable, but in terms of rounded social life it lacks something when compared with a place where school and community are balanced and integrated, such as Castletown or Douglas in the Isle of Man, Thirsk in the North Riding, or the new town of Crawley in Sussex. I recall the London teacher who, concerned at the continued absence of a child from her class, asked the girl's school-friends to call on her and see whether she was ill. But they could not; they did not know where she lived.

A further regrettable consequence of this very limited definition of 'comprehensive' is that more than half of London's new-type schools are for either boys or girls only. In the second half of the twentieth century – when even those dowdy old bodies the universities are thinking of trying out mixed halls of residence – the establishment of new schools on this one-sex basis is deplorable. They can at best be only semi-comprehensive. The real point of the argument for having a school which is a mixed, balanced, healthy, natural community is lost. Such lopsided experience, in an almost exclusively male or female world of up to 2,000 children and adults, cannot be reconciled with the case for an education which is socially complete as well as scholastically sound. On this issue I prefer the Ministry of Education's definition of comprehensive schools as 'schools intended for all secondary pupils in a district' – even though the Ministry, fearful as ever of total commitment, will not allow local authorities to apply it who are eager to do so.

Throughout the period 1944–62 the eleven-plus examination has continued, and on it has been based the allocation of pupils to grammar and technical schools, as well as to the different streams of comprehensive schools. Now at last London proposes to abolish it. But selection will not cease. Instead we shall probably have, as in Anglesey, internal assessment of new pupils in comprehensive schools, and perhaps a special grammar-school entrance examination run by the voluntary grammar schools.

No observer of London's educational scene can fail to be impressed by the size and complexity of the task which faced the county's education committee in 1944 and afterwards, by the zeal with which it has been tackled, and by the degree of success already achieved. Whatever detailed criticisms are made, London's achievement is still a magnificent one. In 1962 there were sixty-eight comprehensive schools, of which forty were in new or substantially new buildings, twenty-eight in old buildings. They provided for nearly two thirds of all the pupils in county secondary schools. Half of London's fifteen-year-olds were deciding to stay at school beyond the minimum leaving age. Since 1958 the Council has been able to guarantee a five-year course to any pupil who desires it. This is a great record by a great administrative service.

3. Inside the Schools

THE doubts concerning comprehensive schools held by the theorists and the men of gold turn on the relative merits of separate types of education on the one hand, common education for all children on the other. Thus the Ministry of Education's first pamphlet, published in 1945, said:

Past experience suggests that schools with a limited and well-defined aim are the most likely to succeed in reaching and maintaining the highest standards within the particular field they serve.

The doubts of the general public are quite different; they practically all turn on fear of one word and its implications: size.

The problem of size

Most adult English people grew up in much smaller societies – towns, villages, schools – than are common today. The Ministry of Education's Chief Inspector of Schools attended a grammar school of 100, which had only three boys in the sixth form. My own grammar school numbered sixty boys when I first went there in 1928. Those of us who are migrants from north to midlands or south cherish a nostalgia for the village in the dales, the sturdy cotton or woollen town with a character of its own and a well-defined compass of geographical and social life. The natives of Warwickshire, Sussex, and so on, while prospering from the boom in work and people and property values, at times feel overwhelmed by the incomers. Many of them wistfully recall the independence of the small trader or craftsman which prevailed in their childhood.

Today's picture is very different. Most grammar schools have from 400 to 800 pupils, most 'modern' schools from 300 to 600. It has, however, been a steady growth, to which people have become accustomed gradually.

Fifteen to twenty years ago, when comprehensive schools first became a public issue, most grammar schools had only 300–500 pupils, most 'modern' schools 100–400. Suddenly the country was confronted with the prospect of new giants which (it was thought) must have at least one thousand pupils to be efficient. A thousand pupils! The figure was the educational equivalent of the sound barrier. (That the barrier was being broken by such respected institutions as Eton College and Manchester Grammar School made little general impact. Such glorious palaces are beyond the ken of common mortals: to us they have the stuff of fairyland or heaven, and therefore we cannot seriously accept them as having any relevance to our daily lives.) Outrage piled on outrage when it appeared that 2,000 rather than 1,000 would be the normal target, if the new schools were to discharge their new role with maximum efficiency. But it's an ill wind that blows no good. Public alarm has made the planners ensure that small social units evolve inside the new communities.

Few would claim complete success for these plans. What new models of houses, cars, refrigerators, find the best answer all at once? And how much more difficult it is to plan for those variable creatures, ourselves! As a Yorkshireman says, 'there's nowt so queer as folk'. Nevertheless, children in comprehensive schools appear to be far more at home, their parents far better pleased and satisfied, than the critics ever expected. Let us look at the present picture.

In the first place, my 1961–2 inquiry showed that the bogy of big schools is not quite so fearsome in reality as it was in anticipation. The biggest comprehensive school has

2,150 pupils, the smallest 160. It is true that the size of a good many of today's comprehensive schools, as of other types of school, is scheduled to rise considerably year by year. If we exclude these, however, sixty-eight of the schools I have studied appear reasonably stable in size. They are distributed as follows:

No. of Schools	No. of Pupils	No. of Schools	No. of Pupils	No. of Schools	No. of Pupils
1	1–200	9	8–900	0	15–1600
0	2–300	3	9–1000	1	16–1700
4	3–400	6	10–1100	0	17–1800
6	4–500	7	11–1200	2	18–1900
5	5–600	3	12–1300	2	19–2000
8	6–700	1	13–1400	1	20–2100
5	7–800	2	14–1500	2	21–2200

This scale does not give a picture of the relative size of *all* comprehensive schools. On the contrary, of the remaining fifty or so surveyed, the great majority were schools which were expected to grow to some point between 1,400 and 2,300. What the scale does show is that there is a large number of established comprehensive schools whose rolls vary evenly from 300 to 1,500. If it can be shown that all such schools are satisfactory, Goliath is slain; there is no longer the need *on educational grounds* for a comprehensive secondary school to be bigger than say 900, though other factors such as shortage of sites may render a larger school necessary or even desirable.

Alas, no such clear-cut generalization seems to me possible. In particularly favourable circumstances, for example with a low pupil/staff ratio and keen parents, a comprehensive school of 500 may be very successful. In other conditions, for example a housing estate where few children stay on at school beyond fifteen, where the parents are apathetic and teachers difficult to obtain, a school of 2,000 may find it all it can do to provide adequate sixth-form education.

But this is a time of rapid growth and change. This chapter is simply a portrait of our comprehensive schools as they move into the mid-sixties; and ten years hence it may well be very different.

The physical environment

In big schools the concourse of some 2,000 children and adults has meant a big challenge to the physical planners of sites and buildings. The physical home of a school is always important, though never so important as the people who inhabit it. On the outskirts of cities some lovely sites have been found, trees have been preserved and planted, architects have often designed gracious buildings. The big headache has been how to reconcile two apparently conflicting needs. On the one hand, space for efficient work, movement, and leisure is needed, room for the individual to breathe and feel uncrowded. On the other, the desire for a school to feel that it is one community calls for buildings compact enough to make communication swift and easy, enabling the head to feel that he is in effective charge, above all ensuring that the children do not feel detached and lost.

In fact, when one thinks of how the buildings – and not only the boarding houses – of great schools like Rugby and Uppingham are scattered over the town, there is by and large little cause for complaint about the layout of comprehensive schools. Of course the architects have sometimes been foolish. A building 180 yards long is as alarming to contemplate as it is tiring to traverse; the lack of covered ways between detached buildings can mean frequent drenching for children and books in wet Wales; cloakrooms may be insufficient at the various points of the school. But most of the obvious defects are the fault not of the architects or the local authority, but of the Government — that is, in the last resort, of ourselves. They are caused by skimping on money, by fearfully costly economy cuts.

In particular, the Ministry's restriction of circulation space by narrowing corridors and stairs or eliminating them altogether, is most unpopular. These schools are busy places. Everyone there has a job to do, and everyone must move about at certain times to the well-equipped rooms where the job can be done best. This is half the point of having such a school at all. No time-and-motion expert would approve the obstacles, the frustration, even the dangers created by squeezing the traffic so that thousands of minutes in all are wasted every day, hundreds of tempers frayed in one such building.

Great stress is laid by educationists on the social aspect and purpose of comprehensive schools. Here again, a mean money policy inhibits gracious living. How can you rehearse a play to your satisfaction in the assembly-cum-dining hall, while tables are being erected and cutlery laid? How can you pipe a sweet note in the music lesson, when the good ladies on the other side of the hatch, bless them, are humming their juke-box selections?

School dinners have been one of the great post-war advances. They were meant to be more than crude canteen eating. Teachers want them to be civilized occasions when teachers and pupils can talk together over food well cooked (as indeed it is) and nicely served (as it often is not), in rooms and with furniture and tableware which lend dignity and atmosphere to the meal.

Other defects are noted. Not uncommon is complaint about the use of too much glass in new schools with a south or south-west aspect, which causes glare and heat from the sun. Too many schools lack soundproofing. All who control spending on school buildings should have the maddening experience of trying to learn or teach in a room loudly invaded by external noises.

Yet, when all fault-finding is done, one's conclusion must be that these are physically fine schools, pretty well-equipped on the whole for the large new job to be tackled in them. And if the quality of materials and workmanship is not always all it might be, we must beware of going to the other extreme and building marble halls which will last for ever. How many secondary-school buildings put up in say 1933–9 are sufficient for the needs of 1963–9? I know of none which is wholly satisfactory, many which are wholly unsatisfactory.

In all seriousness I suggest that our education officers could do much worse than consult Mr Billy Butlin for advice on how to provide, with speed and economy, functional buildings intended to last for no more than twenty years. A healthy economy would thrive on such a policy, and so would our educational ideas. New ideas should command the means, not wait on them. Coventry, with some aluminium-clad buildings, is an authority which has given a lead in this matter. So, too, has the Ministry of Education's own team of architects.

The layout, shape, and size of a school's buildings are particularly important, because they often determine the main framework of a school's internal organization. Such decisions on a new school are almost always made by administrator and architect in consultation; teachers are brought in later to work an already-decided plan. Yet it is the teachers who are the professionals in this sphere of the school's internal daily life. It is highly desirable that the head and some teachers should be appointed a long time in advance and consulted on these questions, though they need not leave their present posts until the new school is ready. Alternatively, the teachers' organizations might set up their own panels of members specially interested in school organization. These panels could take professional advice, and should be consulted on the social and working implications of any new type of school building which might be proposed.

Curriculum and grouping

Because special interests and aptitudes develop as people grow up, a comprehensive school must offer a wide range of possible courses to meet the different needs of different pupils. No English comprehensive school is exactly like any other. Her Majesty's Inspectors of Schools may advise on curriculum and the internal organization of a school, but they cannot dictate; and almost all local education authorities give much freedom to the head of the school in such matters. No actual school, then, corresponds exactly to the description I am about to give. I have tried to present a reasonably accurate composite picture, conveying the essentials without blinding the reader with too much detail and countless qualifications.

An English comprehensive school normally provides a 'foundation course' of either two or three years (ages eleven to thirteen or fourteen) which is followed by all pupils. The usual subjects are: English, mathematics, history, geography, art, handcrafts (boys), housecraft (girls), physical education, music, science, and religion. Religion is the only subject in the curriculum which *must* be provided. French, or another second language, is sometimes studied by all pupils, more often by all except the less able. Latin is usually only begun by the more able pupils.

I say 'less able' and 'more able' because it is the almost universal practice to group incoming pupils *on the basis of general ability* so that the cleverest children learn together, and so on down the scale. This general-ability grouping, known as 'streaming', is usually done on the evidence of the eleven-plus examination, or where no such examination is now held in the district, on the children's performance at the primary school. Out of 102 comprehensive schools recently questioned on this subject, eighty-eight 'stream' the children on entry, eleven during or at the end of the first year. The remaining three do so after two years.

It should be noted that 'streaming' is often in broad blocks rather than finely differentiating one class from another: thus a school which takes in 360 new pupils aged eleven, who have to be divided into twelve classes, may arrange them in four blocks graded A, B, C, and D according to ability, with three parallel forms in each block. Fifteen of the 102 schools questioned have some classes of completely mixed ability, but only four carry such 'unstreamed' classes beyond the third year, and these only in such subjects as crafts, art, music, religion, and physical education.

Further and more accurate grouping according to *ability in particular subjects*, known as 'setting', is usually confined to those pupils already placed in the top third or top half of their age group on general ability. 'Setting' takes place mainly in mathematics, modern languages, English, and science. About half the schools introduce it straightaway with the first-year pupils. Others wait till the second, third, or fourth year. The constant rearrangement of pupils in different groups for different subjects which 'setting' implies, means that it can only be used extensively in a big school with a lot of teachers.

From eleven to thirteen or fourteen, then, there is something approaching a common curriculum in that the various subjects in the foundation course are taken by all or almost all the pupils. The ground covered in each subject, however, varies very widely between the top class and the bottom class of each age group. Individual children are moved up or down the scale according to their progress. The aim is to preserve and enhance the high standards of work which, it is claimed, result from grouping the pupils on ability, while removing the harmful effects, both scholastic and social, which are produced by enforced segregation in separate types of school.

It is extremely difficult to measure the extent of movement between classes from one year to another. The picture is best expressed by a table such as the following, relating to Battersea County School.[1] The composition of each second-year form, numbered vertically on the left, is shown in terms of the number of pupils drawn from each of the first-year forms, numbered horizontally across the top. Thus, for example, the second-year Form 1 (or 'A' stream) contained twenty who had been in the top class the previous year, ten who had been in Form 2 ('B' stream), four from Form 3 ('C' stream), none from Form 4 ('D' stream), and three from Form 5 ('E' stream).

First-year forms 1958-9

		1	2	3	4	5	6	7	8	9
	1	20	10	4		3				
	2	11	13	6	6	1				
	3	3	5	11	10	6	2			
Second-year	4	2	7	10	4	3	8	3		
forms,	5		1	6	8	6	3	4		
1959-60	6				6	7	9	12	2	
	7			3	5	9	12	2	2	
	8				2	3	5	21	5	
	9								4	22

As children grow up, so their special aptitudes emerge more clearly. Pursuing its policy of giving an education suited to the needs of each pupil, the comprehensive school necessarily increases the number and character of different courses available to older pupils. This is done in two main stages. From thirteen or fourteen to sixteen the 'foundation' subjects are continued, but the time given to some of

1. Reproduced from *London Comprehensive Schools*, p. 33.

them is reduced, to others increased, to meet the special interests and needs of different children; and new subjects are introduced as required. The children begin to branch out in different directions, spreading wider as they grow to maturity. This kind of provision is well illustrated by the following table, showing the distribution of fourth-year pupils at Elliott School, London, in 1959–60.[1]

Such provision exceeds in diversity anything a normal grammar or 'modern' school can offer.

The final stage, for those who remain, is from sixteen to nineteen, called in England 'the sixth form'.[2] Hitherto this stage of advanced study has been thought suitable only for that minority of boys and girls whose gifts are intellectual and academic. The comprehensive school certainly provides for them; but in addition it caters for the increasing number of pupils – whose ability may vary from great to small – who seek the benefit of extended secondary education. The number of examination subjects available at this stage is commonly therefore much greater than that provided by the average grammar school. Many comprehensive schools offer close on twenty subjects. For example, one school of 1,300 offers seventeen subjects, including Russian, Spanish, Law, Accountancy, and Technical Drawing. In the rural areas, however, as we have seen, advanced technical and practical courses are too often missing, classes too tiny to be really efficient.

The 'streaming' controversy

Although today's comprehensive schools have settled firmly for classes grouped by ability, it seems probable that this point in their creed will meet with stronger challenge in the future. With the abolition of eleven-plus selection in some areas, more and more junior schools are

1. Reproduced from *London Comprehensive Schools*, p. 43.
2. See pages 52–5 above.

Fourth-year forms, 1959-60	Third-year forms, 1958-9[1]															Total
	1	2	3	4	5	6	7	8	9	10	11	12	13	14	15	
4S Science – Academic	14	12	3													29
K Science – Academic		4	5	2	8	4	3	3	1							30
L Languages – Academic	12	8		1		1	1									23
J Commerce – Academic	1	6	5	6	7	1	2									28
G General Arts – Academic		1	9	8		2	4	5								29
N Engineering – boys		2	4	8	4	6	4	7								35
E Practical – girls			3		4	1	3	2	3	1						17
T Engineering									4	4	6	7	3	6	2	32
U 3 years to 'O' level										5	5	4	6	2	2	24
O Commercial – girls				2	8	4	2		9	1	5					31
F Commercial – boys								3	6	5	3	2	3	4	5	31
R Catering					1	1	2		4	1	3	1	1		1	15
W Woodwork								3	6	3	6	2			6	26
H Horticulture										2	2	2	5			11
V 1 year – Vehicles						1	2	2	3	2	2			5	2	19
Z 1 year – Business				2		3	4	2	3	2	1	4	5	5	2	33
X Christmas leavers						2	2	2		3	5	4	5	5	4	32
Y Easter leavers						3		3	2	5	1	4	4	4	6	32

1. In each case, the numbering of the third-year form is a rough indication of comparative attainment at this stage.

going over to 'unstreamed' classes of mixed ability. This is not terribly revolutionary. It simply means a return to more individual teaching and learning, which operated in my village elementary school (one teacher, thirty children aged five to fourteen) with promotion from one standard to another as you progressed. There is evidence that better results are being achieved as a result by all kinds of children.[1]

But if non-streaming works up to the age of eleven, need it be cut short there? There is every reason to expect that classes of mixed ability will gradually be tried out in the first three years of the secondary school, not merely in 'non-academic' subjects but in the basic subjects too. Beyond fourteen, as the paths of pupils begin to diverge, they have to pick their way by individual choice among a proliferation of courses; and this must mean that personal interest then becomes a prime factor in deciding which group one joins, rather than the grading imposed by the school.

There has been some experiment with classes of mixed ability in comprehensive schools, but it has not gone far. Indeed, London's inspectorate dismisses with scorn the idea that it could or should:

None of the schools bases its organization upon the impracticable assumption that teaching groups covering the whole range of ability are suitable or desirable.[2]

However, they go on to make a comment which is more significant than the authors realize:

1. e.g. J. C. Daniels (*British Journal of Educational Psychology*, XXXI, parts 1 and 2, February and June 1961) concludes (p.127): 'There appears to be fairly definite evidence that the policy of non-streaming, as compared with streaming, significantly increases the average I.Q. of children in the junior school by about three points; ... significantly increases the mean scores of junior school pupils in reading and English tests; ... [and] increases the level of arithmetic attainment of junior school pupils.'

2. *London Comprehensive Schools*, p. 32.

At Woodberry Down ... for about one-third of the timetable, work done in art, music, drama, handicraft, and physical education is in teaching groups of mixed ability. This gives pupils the opportunity to cooperate and to learn together *in subjects where class teaching is at a minimum.*

In what subjects should class teaching *not* be at a minimum ?

One must not be dogmatic about this. Class teaching is often necessary and highly satisfying – curiously enough, I would say especially important in some aspects of physical education (e.g. team games) and music (e.g. orchestra), subjects which in comprehensive schools are usually set aside for mixed ability work. Nor is it wise to try to dragoon teachers into adopting methods which they do not believe in. We must be content to persuade (and be persuaded), never to compel or impose. On the other hand there are undoubtedly academic subjects where the mixing of clever, average, and backward children produces a general fizz, quite different from the flatness of the C stream, so pathetically conscious of their slowness. I have myself frequently taught history and English to classes with a very wide range of ability. One such class included, at one end, a future Ph.D. and a top correspondent of the *Guardian*. They do not seem to have suffered, and I feel sure that pupils of little ability in such classes benefited more than the children segregated in lower streams whom I have taught elsewhere.

Much stronger testimony comes from the carefully-documented work of A. W. Rowe[1] with classes of mixed ability. It is true that he works in 'modern' schools which lack the most able children. His principles cannot be fully applied. But no one who inspects the day-to-day work of children and staff in his school can fail to acknowledge the quality of the individual work being done, can doubt that

1. *The Education of the Average Child* (Harrap, 1960).

grammar-school children too would benefit by the wide-spread adoption of his methods. Indeed, the best sixth-form teachers have always practised them.

Rowe's approach demands tremendously thorough pre-paration of material by the teacher, and equally thorough forethought about how this material can be used effectively by the different individuals in his class. Learning will often take place singly or in groups, although there are occasions when the whole class is brought together and everyone's attention focused on one topic. When you go into such a classroom you see first the people who matter – the children, busily concentrating on their particular jobs. Only then do you notice the teacher, quietly discussing a point with this child, or that group, moving around unobtrusively. How different from the dominant figure of old, declaiming on his dais at the front! Yet the change should not really surprise us. We take the more civilized methods for granted at the two extremes of our school system, in the infant school and the sixth form. As we have observed, they are spreading into the junior school. Rowe cracks the toughest nut of all. If they work successfully in the 'modern' school, as he has proved, they will work anywhere.

What we need, then, is flexibility in our grouping of children and in our teaching of them. The essential point is well made by Professor Tibble:

Unless we start ... with the individual nature of the learning process and the varied needs of individual children, and relate our means and methods in a thoroughgoing way to this, we are producing but palliatives. It means placing the emphasis on learning not teaching, on the provision of incentives and occasions and materials for learning rather than on teaching methods and skills. The role and skill of the teacher is then not less important, but it is different, and certainly not less difficult. In Mr Rowe's words, 'he no longer imposes; he evokes'.[1]

Examination performances: the General Certificate of Education

The report on *Early Leaving* indicated that eight and a half per cent of the full eleven-plus age-group who entered secondary schools maintained by local authorities in 1946 had six and a half years later gained five or more passes at the ordinary level of GCE, or had reached an equivalent standard. Five passes is commonly reckoned a good performance. In the words of the North Riding education committee's annual report for 1959, they are 'the basic preliminary requirement for most professional and equivalent occupations'.

An unpublished inquiry among sixteen counties and thirty county boroughs in 1959 by W. R. Smedley suggested that there had been a small improvement in this respect since 1953. Adopting a more stringent criterion than that used in *Early Leaving*, Smedley found that, on average, eight and a half per cent of all children entering local secondary schools were gaining five or more passes five (not six) years later. Inquiries which I made in 1962 indicated that performance had continued to rise. In fifty-two local education authorities the proportion gaining a 'good' GCE, as defined above, ranged from seven to fourteen per cent, with ten per cent the most common figure. Seven other returns fell outside the general range, mainly below it.[2]

We may reasonably conclude, then, that in the local secondary schools of England and Wales as a whole, a

1. *Forum*, 11, 1, pp. 8–9.
2. Figures from local education authorities which send a substantial proportion of children to independent or direct-grant schools have been excluded.

system based mainly on separate grammar and 'modern' schools, about ten per cent of each age-group proceed to take a 'good' GCE around the age of sixteen.

Only two areas in Britain are completely comprehensive: the Isle of Man and Anglesey. Culturally they have no special advantages. Nevertheless, in the Isle of Man on average sixteen and a half per cent of the relevant age-group gained a 'good' GCE during the four years 1959-62. In Anglesey the average for 1959-61 was over fourteen per cent. In those Welsh counties other than Anglesey where a large number of the schools are comprehensive, the proportion gaining 'good' GCEs is impressive; during 1958-61 the average for Cardiganshire was twenty-one per cent. The orthodox local education authority which most closely approaches the latter figure is East Sussex, which averaged over eighteen per cent for 1959-61. It may be significant that there are GCE courses in all the 'modern' schools of this county. This naturally enlarges the opportunity for all children to show that they can do well in external examinations.

To supplement these figures, I inquired of twenty comprehensive schools in various parts of the country concerning the later GCE performance of the pupils who had joined them at the age of eleven in 1954. Several of these schools were quite heavily creamed by grammar schools. Even so, fourteen per cent of the age-group in question gained a 'good' GCE. The same figure, fourteen per cent, emerges from a table compiled by the Secondary School Examinations Council in 1961, based on returns from five comprehensive schools.[1]

Such evidence as we have, then, suggests that whereas a system of separate types of secondary school normally produces around ten per cent of each age-group getting

1. *The Certificate of Secondary Education* (H.M.S.O., 1961), pp.19-20.

'good' GCEs after five years, comprehensive schools are normally achieving about fourteen per cent. This is a significant improvement. It bears out a simple thesis: that selection at eleven is premature and inaccurate, and cannot be wholly put right by a makeshift attempt at later transfers; and that if one keeps open the door of full opportunity, many more children will pass through it.

However, it should not be concluded that substantial further improvement is not possible or likely. I have found eleven comprehensive schools which in this or that year have exceeded twenty per cent.

A particularly impressive record is that of Mellow Lane, a Middlesex school of 1,120 girls and boys and fifty-six teachers, which serves the industrial area of Hayes. It is handicapped by poor buildings, and loses the cream of the local eleven-plus entry to grammar schools; yet its record of 'good' GCE results during the four years 1959–62, expressed as a percentage of successive age groups, averages twenty-one and a half per cent. And Mellow Lane is far from being a sweatshop. It has a big range of social activities. Small wonder that in nine years no fewer than eleven members of staff have gone to be heads of schools elsewhere.

The figures for results in the advanced level examinations of GCE show that in sixth-form work comprehensive schools compare not unfavourably with the orthodox English system.

In 1962 I found that, in the schools of fifty-two local education authorities, from three to eight per cent of the age-group who had been admitted to secondary schools seven years earlier passed in two or more subjects at advanced level. The most common figure (fifteen authorities) was four per cent, but the average of the authorities' figures – not, however, a weighted average to take account of differences in school population – was five and a half per cent.

In the Isle of Man during 1959–62 eight and a half per cent attained comparable results. The only other completely comprehensive area, Anglesey, averaged over seven per cent during 1959–61. Returns from the twenty comprehensive schools in different parts of England and Wales, whose results for the ordinary level of GCE have already been quoted, indicated that on average six per cent passed in two or more subjects at the advanced level of GCE.

The evidence here is less substantial, both for the national picture and for comprehensive schools, than it is with regard to the ordinary level of GCE. So far as it goes, it suggests that sixth-form work in comprehensive schools, as measured by advanced-level results, is at least as successful as that in a system of selective schools. It has not yet, however, established the clear superiority which they seem to have in GCE ordinary level examinations.

Only in the winning of university scholarships in England, though not in Wales, have the comprehensive schools failed to make much impact. This is no doubt largely due to the fact that in England nearly all the most highly intelligent boys and girls still go to grammar schools. Contacts with Oxford and Cambridge are extremely slender. From twenty schools which had had a sixth form for two years or more – the maximum was ten years – by 1961–2 only ten pupils had gone to Oxbridge, although at least 325 had gone to other universities.

Obviously more time is required to build up really good sixth forms, and results so far are encouraging. They may be better still as the new, big comprehensives get into their stride. First results from one such school show that thirty-three candidates gained sixteen distinctions and sixty-seven passes at advanced level. Three boys won State scholarships, three 'eleven-plus failures' each gained three advanced level passes and a university place. In all, twelve students won places at universities, five places at colleges of advanced technology, and four places at teachers' training colleges.

On the other hand, there is no doubt that advanced work in some comprehensive schools suffers because they are 'creamed' by grammar schools. There are therefore some attractions in a policy which would concentrate all sixth-form work in grammar schools. This is the work which interests them most and which they probably do best. Croydon might be content to recruit to such grammar schools at fifteen or sixteen, Leicestershire at thirteen or fourteen.

Some local authorities might still believe a seven-year run in the grammar school from eleven-plus to be desirable for some children. Even here, however, if GCE ordinary level examinations can be taken in all other types of secondary school, as is already the case in East Sussex, Hastings, Bournemouth, and Warwickshire, and is planned in Surrey, something worth while is being achieved.

Sometimes, however, there are drawbacks in transferring 'modern' school pupils at sixteen to the sixth form of a grammar school with the normal age-range, whose own pupils are established and who may not always welcome the newcomers. One such transferred boy, who later took a university degree, told me:

We were regarded as inferior, and to some extent felt it – both academically, where end-of-term examinations found us occupying the lower half of the form lists, and socially, which we were in fact. One of the grammar-school sixth-form later said that at first they just could not understand us or why we refused to accept their principles and ideals. Although eventually coming to respect us for our academic ability, they could never really like us. 'Well,' he said, 'you were different.'

Finally, a word on the child who gains fewer than five passes at ordinary level. When the Secondary School Examinations Council in 1951 replaced the old 'grouped' School Certificate by individual subject certificates, it recognized that even one success at GCE level might be valuable to a boy or girl, both materially and as a morale-booster. Today's comprehensive schools commonly have one third of their pupils gaining one to four passes; and occasionally the proportion rises to one half.

If we believe in growth – and who, in education, cannot? – in the light of this evidence we should be unwise to draw any precise line of recruitment to GCE courses. The only practical solution is to establish GCE courses in *all* secondary schools.

Eleven-plus 'failures'

It is no longer necessary to amass examples of children who fail to get to a grammar school at eleven and later make good. The serious weaknesses of selection at eleven are now accepted.

Nevertheless we must not forget that this selection process is going on all the time, and that it has very serious consequences for individual people. Ministers and chief education officers may take a grand view twenty years ahead, but this is little help to the child who is now eleven years old. When I mention the following random examples of late development in our few comprehensive schools, I really have in mind the army of nameless ones who could have come up likewise, but have been lost in the quicksands of our selective system.

In 1961, 126 boys from the first comprehensive intake of 413 entered the sixth form of a London boys' school, sixty-two of them to study academic courses. These sixty-two came from no fewer than nine of the original thirteen first-year forms – that is, some from well below the ability average as assessed at eleven. A neighbouring London girls' school has a similar record.

In a Home Counties school in 1961, four of the five university places obtained were won by boys who had failed the eleven-plus, and one of these won a State scholarship. The head of the same school adds:

I have identical twins in the school, one of whom failed and one who passed the eleven-plus. Both are now in a 'grammar' form and occupy second and third positions respectively.

At Bristol, seventeen comprehensive school pupils who had failed the eleven-plus secured twenty-six advanced level passes among them in 1961. Six of them were accepted by universities, including one at Cambridge.

The head boy of a north midlands school in 1961–2 was one of several eleven-plus failures who went on to take GCE at advanced level. A head girl in Liverpool, who failed both the eleven-plus and the thirteen-plus examinations, gained six GCE passes at ordinary level and was accepted for training college at the age of seventeen. Elsewhere the examples of late development in comprehensive schools abound: John, whose I.Q. was 91, gaining five GCE passes at ordinary level: Jack, I.Q. 103, gaining six passes; Jean, an eleven-plus failure who gained eight ordinary-level passes before taking three advanced-level science subjects; James, who had failed to get into not only a grammar school but a central (intermediate) school, gaining six passes; Andrew, who came from the bottom stream of a central school, passing advanced-level GCE in history and mathematics, adding economics later, and now at a university; David, an eleven-plus failure, going on to win a Trevelyan Scholarship at Christ Church, Oxford; a whole group of eight boys at one school, all eleven-plus failures with moderate I.Q.s, who have averaged six GCE ordinary-level passes in such subjects as English, mathematics, physics, chemistry, history, and geography, and are now in the sixth form.

A school in the west of England, which opened in 1957 with only one form of 'selected' pupils, reported:

Nevertheless eleven candidates took GCE in July 1961, four of them 'modern' pupils – all of the eleven under sixteen, and one under fourteen. They passed in forty-five out of fifty-five subjects, including Latin and German.

In a midlands comprehensive school, 107 pupils gained at least one GCE pass in 1961; forty-two of them had failed the eleven-plus. Five of the twenty-six who gained at least five passes were eleven-plus failures.

It would be tedious to go on. There is overwhelming evidence that the comprehensive schools are giving justice, in so far as that is possible, to children whose early progress has been held back. And yet ... how far there is to go! The head of one comprehensive school in the west, himself a distinguished university scholar and educationist, says:

After extensive inquiries, I have not found any pupil who failed the eleven-plus who has overcome his sense of inferiority at this failure, irrespective of his performance even at university level.

If that is so with the exceptions who fight their way back, how much deeper is the humiliation of those who, through no fault of their own, must for ever accept that early stamp: 'Inferior quality – reject.' It is specious to argue that all have the chance to reverse an adverse verdict at eleven-plus. The selective system is so constructed that only a minority of children can ever join the elect; there must always be a majority who are cast out.

The worry and tension created in so many homes before the examination are harmful enough. The after-effects of failure are very much worse. They are obvious when one member of a family succeeds and another fails. They are, however, just as hurtful to any child who is dismissed as unworthy – and despite all the plausible arguments in favour of selection, that is how children and parents see it.

Those who are most deeply hurt usually assume a poker face to hide the wound. It is not healed in a matter of months or even years. Many young people react by revolting against the society which has spurned them. Crime mounts every year. Adolescents are punished for seemingly senseless acts of destruction, with no noticeable effect. The hidden offenders, however, are ourselves – we who persist in social and educational policies both cruel and futile, if more refined than the things in *Oliver Twist* and *The Water Babies* which now horrify us.

The various churches profess to follow a teacher who fiercely attacked all such distinctions damaging to human dignity. Today they are worried because many people, though still insisting that they are Christians, have lost faith in the leadership of clergymen; yet each as a body does nothing about our own form of *apartheid*, the compulsory segregation of young children in different types of school. Here is a social evil which the Christian church ought not to tolerate for a moment.

Although there is no concerted action, some clergy are very conscious of the basic flaws in our society. Writing with rare insight in an article about Oxford-Borstal camps, the Rev. J. N. Jory puts his finger on the essential point.

We are always giving each other labels, categorizing, classifying and then thinking that we have simplified our problem, that we know where we stand. In creating such categories we only deceive ourselves, and sometimes hinder those who strive to live happy and purposeful lives. God made people, we have often sought to label them. . . .

We changed the word delinquency to need. The need of every boy to know that he 'belonged' to somebody, that decency and happiness are bound up together. . . . Need so many-sided that it spells poverty. We cannot expect penitence in those who look back in anger, and we ought to ask ourselves: 'Is the poverty of the age due to my greed, my blindness, my withholding?' . . .

The restoration of self-respect, essential to every offender who has been humiliated by our society and yet seeks to live a life of dignity and decency, can only come through other people; people willing to accept him, have confidence in him and give him the opportunity to express himself.[1]

I have stressed here the human wrong done by compulsory segregation at eleven-plus, because that is by far the most important consideration. Those who harden their hearts, however, may possibly be convinced by the material aspect, by the need to use every person's talent to its fullest capacity. That depends on everyone feeling that he counts, and that he is capable of doing important work which is valued by others. It also requires us to pursue a policy of full opportunity and encouragement in schools, instead of restricted opportunity and discouragement, which we have at present. All who are concerned about national output and the quality of British workmanship should consider very hard whether the shortcomings they deplore do not have their origins in a school system which automatically dashes the self-respect of the majority of children, and for some destroys it.

Less able children

Examinations, of course, are by no means confined to GCE. I have concentrated on that because it is a standard nationally accepted and understood outside schools, and the only one in which objective comparisons can be made between the records of different types of school.

In fact the comprehensive schools run a wide range of courses for children of around-average ability, such as those shown in the earlier table of fourth-year work at Elliott School. They lead to a range of fifth-year examinations and certificates almost as wide – Royal Society of Arts, College of Preceptors, Union of Educational Institutions,

1. *Yorkshire Post*, 13 July 1961.

Union of Lancashire & Cheshire Institutes, Northern Counties Technical Examinations, etc. – not to mention the local Certificate, usually taken after four years, which a number of education authorities and divisional executives have introduced.

All these have served a useful purpose, but some tidying-up was clearly needed. The Beloe Committee, in September 1960, recommended an external examination taken after five years and organized by some twenty regional examining boards. The Secondary School Examinations Council has accordingly proposed the establishment of a new Certificate of Secondary Education for children who cannot reach GCE standard. The Minister, while accepting the main proposition, is rightly reluctant to put the development of this work in a strait-jacket, and awaits further advice from his Advisory Council on the best kind of education for children in the middle and lower groups.

Beloe assumed that the top twenty per cent of an age-group would take GCE, and that the new lower certificate would cater for the next forty per cent, leaving a bottom forty per cent for whom any examination was considered undesirable. However, the figures given earlier suggest that thirty to fifty per cent will attempt GCE, and that rising standards may encourage perhaps another thirty per cent from those in the lower band to attempt the new CSE in individual subjects at least.

The large size of many comprehensive schools enables them to make much-needed special provision for backward children. Specially trained teachers are appointed – when they can be found. Backward children are commonly grouped in small classes under such teachers, and not taught by subject specialists. The school's aim is not to detach the backward child from a normal environment for his whole school life, but to help him to master the basic skills of reading and number, to dispel emotional blocks, and to fit him to resume his place in a normal class at the earliest possible moment. Some schools prefer to leave the backward child in a normal class and withdraw him only for special tuition during certain periods.

While quite a lot is being done in remedial teaching, provision for psychological guidance is less satisfactory. It is right that we should expect our teachers to be more than mere classroom specialists, that they should care for the general welfare of their pupils. But in a disturbed society such as ours, with divorce and movement from one community to another as commonplaces, there are great emotional stresses on many children. We need here to follow America, as in so many other matters, by establishing guidance departments headed by trained people in every large secondary school, or alternatively in area groups of junior and senior high schools.

Children's attitudes

How attractive and worthwhile does the comprehensive school seem to the pupils? Despite being, as Napoleon said, ' a nation of shopkeepers', we are too patriarchal really to accept that the customer is always right. So it has been left to an Australian, Dr T. W. G. Miller, to investigate pupils' attitudes and consider the question of values from their point of view.[1]

Miller's study related to boys aged thirteen to fourteen. In three different parts of England he compared the attitudes of boys in grammar schools on certain matters with those of boys in comprehensive schools (termed 'comprehensive grammar' below) whose abilities and home backgrounds were similar. He likewise compared similar groups in 'modern' and comprehensive schools ('comprehensive modern' below). His most significant conclusions were these:

1. *Values in the Comprehensive School* (Oliver and Boyd, 1961).

1. The 'comprehensive grammar' boys had a very slightly higher proportion of active leisure-time interests (e.g. playing rather than watching football) than the boys from separate grammar schools. Third came the 'comprehensive modern' groups, a bad last those from 'modern' schools.

2. The group which had the highest opinion of its own school was 'comprehensive modern'; second came 'comprehensive grammar', third grammar school, fourth 'modern' school. At the same time the boys' estimate of their school's standing in the eyes of the public was realistic: 1. grammar school; 2. comprehensive school; 3. 'modern' school.

3. 'Comprehensive grammar' and 'comprehensive modern' together had the highest opinion of the *courses* offered by their schools. Grammar school and 'modern' school came lower, and close together.

4. Tests of 'morale' and attitude to schooling and education generally (e.g. homework) produced this order: 1. 'comprehensive grammar' closely followed by grammar school – the difference was scarcely significant; 3. 'comprehensive modern'; 4. 'modern' school.

5. Finally, all the boys were asked: 'Do you wish to leave school as soon as possible?' The answer 'No' came as follows: 'comprehensive grammar' ninety-three per cent; grammar school eighty-three per cent; 'comprehensive modern' seventy-two per cent; 'modern' school fifty-seven per cent.

Miller's work shows very clearly that the comprehensive schools are already meeting pupils' needs which in a divided secondary system are generally unsatisfied. It further shows that they are encouraging a bigger proportion to stay longer at school, learning to use their talents to the full. One of the most significant features of his findings is that even in the 'modern' schools, where pupils clearly felt themselves and the school to be inferior, more than half wanted to continue their education. There is an enormous unsatisfied demand for higher secondary education: a significant reserve of talent thirsting for full nourishment and training. Crowther found that two out of five of our ablest boys leave school by the age of sixteen. This situation must be remedied.

Staying on at school

The Ministry of Education's published statistics do not show the proportions of each age group who stay at school for a full fifth, sixth, or seventh year. However, from the numbers given for different ages it is possible to make rough calculations. In January 1961 about thirty per cent of their respective age-groups (in maintained schools only) would complete a fifth year, fifteen per cent a sixth year, and seven per cent a seventh year.[1]

What is the position in comprehensive schools? Naturally there is a good deal of variation, depending partly on the sort of local society served by the school, partly on how long the school has been in existence, and partly on how far it is 'creamed' by grammar and independent schools. During 1961–2 returns from comprehensive schools showed that from half to two thirds of their pupils commonly stayed for a fifth year, between ten and twenty per cent normally stayed for a sixth year, and between five and fifteen per cent normally stayed for a seventh year. In each case, however, some individual schools were achieving much higher proportions. In 1960–1 the percentage staying for a full fifth year at Wandsworth comprehensive school was just under seventy per cent, at Haverstock sixty per cent, at Forest Hill fifty-five per cent, at Elliott about fifty per cent, and at Peckham about forty-five per cent. Some other schools, growing from former 'modern' or central schools, have much lower figures, but the fifth and sixth forms are steadily building up.

1. *Statistics of Education, 1961*, Pt I, Table 24, shows that 35% of the relevant age-group stayed at school to age 15, 18% to 16, 9% to 17, 3% to 18.

The general picture, as one might expect, is similar to that given by our survey of examination results. Proportionately, twice as many young people are staying on to sixteen in comprehensive schools as under the segregated system, but after that age the overall figures are very similar. In view of their very recent origin, this sixth-form picture in the comprehensive schools is encouraging.

There are two possible reasons why pupils are staying longer at comprehensive schools. One is simply that these schools offer a more efficient service. They provide more courses. Late developers, too, who would otherwise be sent at eleven to a 'modern' school with perhaps no GCE or other examination courses, are able to move up to the examination forms quite easily.

The other possibility is that the school itself may be a more attractive society to live in than is the average 'modern' school or even a selective grammar school. Miller's findings suggest that this is true also. But if it is so, why? Are the teaching methods very different from those practised in grammar and/or 'modern' schools? Are the incentives to learning more attractive, or the deterrents to laziness and misbehaviour more effective? What sort of a society is it to live in?

Teaching methods

The first point can be dismissed very quickly. The teachers in comprehensive schools are nearly all grammar-school products who have previously taught in either grammar or 'modern' schools. All too often, then, practices familiar in the grammar school appear; much chalk and talk, a good deal of note-dictating, coaching for 'spotted' questions in forthcoming examinations, frequent tests which demand more of memory than understanding. 'Modern' schools, too, under-staffed and over-worked, are by no means free from such methods. Such teaching is bad for all children, but the clever ones can pick up something. That does not apply to the less able children, and many heads of departments in comprehensive schools sometimes have to re-educate themselves and their assistants painfully by trial and error.

On the other hand, in the comprehensive situation the former 'modern' teacher's practical approach, the former 'grammar' teacher's disciplined approach, are sometimes merged. Both teachers can learn from each other, to the benefit of all pupils.

English comprehensive schools practise 'streaming by ability'. Whatever its advantages, one snag is that it encourages all but the best teachers to rely on formal class teaching rather than on flexible and often individual work. Although the latter appears here and there, particularly with retarded children, it is not noticeably more common in comprehensive than in 'modern' and grammar schools.

2. THE SCHOOL AS A SOCIETY AND IN SOCIETY

The headmaster

L'état, c'est moi. One of the sharpest differences I have noticed between schools in England and those across the Atlantic is that in the status and role of the headmaster (and headmistress). Over there it is felt that the school belongs to the local community, which has a real say in what goes on. The head has an important part to play, but he is still just one of the team.

In England it is quite different. The head (I speak of all types of school) is king of the castle, and any discussions parents may have with him on the running of the school are by grace and favour, not as of right. We have to contend with two kinds of autocracy: that of the local authority, which decides in its wisdom which type of school a child should go to, and that of the headmaster.

Even when, as is beginning to happen a little more, parents are given an effective say about the kind of school most suitable for their child, their participation too often ends at the school door. It is far from unusual for a child to be put into one course or denied admission to another without reference to the parents. In the late seventeenth century Dr Busby, headmaster of Westminster, refused to remove his hat when King Charles II visited the school, lest his pupils should suspect that there was any man greater than himself. That tradition has persisted. 'I mean to be boss in my own school' is a familiar phrase. But *is* it 'his' school?

This does not mean that head teachers in general are lacking in concern for their pupils' welfare: not at all. They are, if anything, too possessive, too impatient of the parents' views, so sure that they know best that they prefer where possible to take unilateral action. It is true that they proclaim, with one voice, that a parent can always come to see them about his child; but not infrequently a parent's doubts really turn on aspects of the school's organization, attitudes, and methods which require general appraisal before the individual case can be fully understood. There are parents' evenings, open days, and so on; but full, free, organized discussion of the fundamental principles and practices on which the school stands is as rare as snow in summer. It *can* happen; how rarely it does!

This is the background against which we must view the head of the English comprehensive school today. One must not expect a revolution overnight. Changing a framework is one thing, changing attitudes of mind quite another. What we see, in fact, is an impressive concern for the individual child. The fear that a comprehensive-school head must be a remote impersonal figure is not borne out. Indeed, in some ways he is better able to interest himself in people than can heads of smaller schools. But his rule, though always benevolent, is still paternal.

To some extent this stems from the organization of the large school. Coventry's pattern of various buildings, grouped on a common campus, seems to embody the basic concept of the English comprehensive school – diversity within a greater unity. It also calls for a larger view of the role of the head – a view familiar to us, in fact, in the bigger 'public' schools. The head becomes a kind of prime minister, *primus inter pares*, working closely with a band of responsible senior colleagues – heads of houses and/or of lower and upper schools, and heads of departments.

He is assisted by an administrative staff which is under an officer of experience and personal quality, a man or woman capable of assuming major responsibilities. This is one of London's many contributions to English school organization, though it is of course already common in America.

It would be petty and inefficient if the headmaster attempted the detailed running of the school, as the head of a small school has to do. His concern is at once larger and more intimate, and may be classified under the three Ps: (1) policy and planning; (2) public relations outside the school – particularly important in a school which is, or should be, *par excellence* a school for the community; (3) personal relations inside the school. Relief from administrative chores frees the head to use his special personal qualities in making direct contact with all the staff, and for contacts with some pupils too – for example in societies, the school council, and an occasional lesson. At the top, therefore, the comprehensive school needs precisely the kind of democratic leadership, warm, wise, and balanced, which is needed at the helm of a college, a university, or a boarding school.

All this is fine in theory. The critics, however, have

repeatedly suggested that there are not enough teachers capable of doing this job well. Sir Edward Boyle, for example, said in 1959: 'It is the Government's view, and I am sure this is right, that only the very exceptional head teacher can infuse a spirit of unity into a school of say 2,000 pupils.'[1] Partly this view arises from the discredited but persistent belief that the pool of ability is small and limited. Partly, perhaps, it indicates a certain unconscious arrogance among some of those who have come to eminent positions in society, and who can no longer accept the idea that they are not such rare mortals after all.

Judgement in such matters must always be personal, so no case can be proved one way or the other. If my own comment is worth anything, it is only because over the years my work has brought me into contact with a large number of teachers and administrators in schools, universities, and colleges, including many headmasters and headmistresses. Where one is taken for granted and, like Father Brown's postman, an ordinary person calling for no special show, an accurate opinion is perhaps more likely to be formed.

In 1954 I wrote of one small comprehensive school and its headmaster:

It must not be thought that Castle Rushen is extremely 'progressive' ... Its virtues are the virtues of moderation, balance, and a liberal attitude of mind. Mr Cretney prefers leading by the hand to pushing and pulling; example to exhortation ... In his care to hasten slowly he has introduced some [traditional] practices which will be difficult to uproot. But it must be conceded that they are largely compensated by personal attention to every child.[2]

Of course, all headmasters and headmistresses have different qualities. Nevertheless my overall picture of com-

1. *Education*, 23 January 1959, p. 154.
2. *Education*, 7 May 1954, pp. 791–2.

prehensive-school heads comes increasingly near to that description. They are sincere, devoted men and women, aware of detail and of individuals in their schools, but not to the exclusion of wider ideas. They are not much interested in publicity. In present circumstances this may be a weakness, for the goods they have for sale merit greater public understanding. Better this, however, than to sound the trumpets from the start onwards, long before the new order has had time to prove itself, as a status-conscious administrator or politician may sometimes be tempted to do.

The staff

These heads, whose general calibre is impressive, are drawn largely from the ranks of teachers who have served in separate types of school. Younger men and women are now appearing, however, whose liberal sympathies and administrative gifts have taken them into responsible posts in comprehensive and similar schools. Behind them throng many good candidates.

The real problem is not finding enough good heads, but ensuring a satisfying, sufficiently responsible position for the many who are capable of being good heads but who will never get the opportunity. As schools – all types of schools – get bigger, and more teachers are recruited, the chances of promotion to headships get less. If we stick to rat-race rules, we shall have fierce competition for the top posts, possibly distorting the values of assistant teachers, disturbing the harmony of what should be a happy co-operating community, and producing a growing number of dispirited men who count themselves failures.

A staff of thirty to a hundred teachers is a body of unusually gifted people. All are important, and it is necessary that all should feel important (in a responsible, not vain, sense) if they are to give of their best. What happens now?

In the big comprehensive school there is usually a hierarchy of senior members of staff. The headmaster has his cabinet of deputies, heads of houses and heads of departments. Outside the magic circle are the other assistant teachers, who have little direct say in policy. It is true that periodic staff meetings are usually held, and that questions of major policy may be discussed there. There are also meetings of house staff and department staff, to consider detailed matters affecting those sections; and a good school will also have its senior-commonroom committee, elected regardless of official status. But a large meeting is a poor substitute for a round-table gathering when thrashing out the finer points of some important issue; and transmission of one's point of view through a head of department is uncertain, unsatisfying, and liable to lose much of its conviction when conveyed (if it is properly conveyed) at second hand.

The fault mainly lies in the promotion ladder built up by successive Burnham reports: a series of graded posts for which teachers must compete, which has caused hard feelings and bad relations in many staff rooms. This system puts a premium on ability to organize, whereas one might have thought that ability to teach was the most precious quality of all.

What we need in schools is a recognition that all members of staff are doing work so important that financial differentiation between them *on the basis of work as such* cannot reasonably be made. Experience, which all acquire as the years go by, is a different matter, and can be fairly assessed. So can extra years of training and higher qualifications, which one would wish to encourage.

There is much to be said for an academic community which rates classroom teaching as high as anything else, and passes round the administrative jobs in turn, so that in due course all experience and benefit from a share in the inner councils. Some may appear at first sight less suited to this than others; but people do tend to grow with the job. Human beings are adaptable, as educationists should be the first to recognize. Capacity to learn is not confined to the pupils. The larger benefits to the happiness and unity of the staff could be immense.

Democracy in school

I have observed that the teachers in our comprehensive schools are themselves the products of grammar schools, and that their experience has usually been in grammar or 'modern' schools. It is not surprising, then, to find that apart from the quite limited belief that secondary-school children should not be segregated in separate types of school, these teachers have transplanted into the new schools almost all the standard grammar-school attitudes to children's education.

Take, for example, prefects: an élite of older children, who help in the running of the school and the control of other pupils. I am not one of those who believe that children do not need the guiding hand of authority at all; far from it. The business of education is fundamentally that of gradually changing the helpless immature baby, completely dependent on adult authority, into the capable, mature, free adult. It is a long process. Control eventually gives way to guidance, guidance gives way to advice; and conversely the growing child assumes increasing responsibilities for both himself and others. It is right that older pupils should take an increasing share in the internal government of the school. But the need and the right to have this experience belong to *all* children at the appropriate point for their social group, not just to a select few.

Conservative-minded critics think this concern for education in social democracy is irrelevant to the purpose of the comprehensive school. H. C. Dent, for example, writes:

One thing at a time. The comprehensive principle itself offers a sufficiently large, difficult, and exciting field for experiment; do not further complicate the task of those who are adventuring in it by including elements which, however attractive, are essentially extraneous.[1]

In fact this business of selecting and elevating a few, rejecting and excluding the mass, is at least as important in a school's social life as in the classroom. It goes to the heart of our educational and social philosophy. Yet no fewer than ninety-six out of a hundred schools of which I have inquired have prefects: in seventy chosen by head and/or staff, in three by older pupils, in twenty-three by some combination of staff and pupils.

On the other hand there is light at the end of the tunnel in that in some schools the prefect system is very broadly based. For example, one headmaster says: 'All the sixth are considered responsible elder brethren.' The fifth form there have one year's prefect duty, and house prefects drawn from the third and fourth years each do a fortnight's duty. The aim is to spread responsibility very widely through the school. Another school, similarly, has no upper-school prefects, but prefects in the lower and middle school. These are examples of the moderate, liberal, far-sighted policy to which I referred earlier. The old trappings remain; but within, new growth and fresh ideas are slowly and quietly beginning to transform the scene.

Few have a School Council elected by some or all of the children; and the powers of those that do exist are modest. Where they are being tried, people are pleased with them. In one small school of 400, for example, the children are found to be remarkably upright and detached about choosing the best representatives, and stooges are rare. Sometimes the elected children learn to administer

1. Essay in *Comprehensive Schools Today* (Councils and Education Press, 1955), p. 40.

money wisely – an excellent experience. There is much to be said for giving the older pupils, at least, training in democratic procedures and responsibilities in this way, and nothing serious to be said against it. Don't we want more people to vote and take an active part in local government?

The explanation, I fear, is simply that teachers are not much interested in this question. Their attitude is merely negative, not obstructive; they are happy to see children from different streams and different kinds of home mixing socially. Only a few have thought out a philosophy and, arising from it, methods designed to produce an actively cooperating society and the conditions which would make comprehensive schools vehicles of a communal culture. Among the exceptions are certain London schools, where interest in the social value of comprehensiveness is probably more lively than anywhere else. At Walworth, for example, in the O'Reilly tradition, they are still 'concerned with the ideal of intelligent participation by all on "a democratic basis rather than producing quotas of leaders" '.[1]

Other features of today's comprehensive schools confirm this general picture. As a body they vary from moderately conservative to cautiously liberal, with rare flashes of radicalism here and there. Their attitude to the wearing of school uniform is typical of much else. Every one of a hundred schools which I questioned about this has a school uniform; on the other hand, though all are encouraged to wear it, the policy is applied with sympathy and tolerance. Upper-school girls often have considerable latitude, with some individual choice of style or colour. At least one school allows the older girls to wear make-up, and all girls to wear jewellery in moderation.

It is possible that much of the outrageous make-up and dress flaunted by teenagers is produced by the need to revolt against authoritarian school standards. Might it not

1. *London Comprehensive Schools*, p. 28.

be better if more schools did what a few already do – deal with personal health, beauty, taste, and design in an appropriate part of the curriculum? *Shoppers' Guide* and *Which?* have begun to educate the middle-class adult, to rescue him from the domination of commercial advertising. But only the schools, and I think particularly the comprehensive schools, can teach the whole nation that self-determination in this matter is both possible and desirable.

Limited freedom in an approved area can be most frustrating. We are so often saying: 'Do what you like, apart from the thing you most want to do.' Young men and women can only become free by practising freedom. I have already said that they are not yet ready for complete freedom; but I believe that this area, of dress and personal appearance, is one for which they *are* ready, one which concerns most of them enormously, and which we should use to ease the gradual transition of responsibility to their own shoulders. They must bear it all very very soon. On such matters as dress, taste, and etiquette we can move earlier into our future role of friendly advisers.

Incentives

The traditional picture fills out when we turn to incentives in comprehensive schools. Of a hundred schools, eighty-nine give their children ranking orders in class, either overall positions (1st, 5th, 30th, and so on) or positions for particular subjects only. Eleven schools, however, do not, because as one of these heads says: 'We encourage boys to better their own previous best, rather than to compete with each other.' Further, seventy-nine of the eighty-nine schools make known the children's class positions, whether overall or for separate subjects, to all the children in the class concerned. Only three schools make these ranking orders known only to the children's parents, privately. Seven keep the information for the teachers' use only.

The award of prizes or trophies is widely practised: eighty-seven schools give them for academic work, eighty-nine for games and athletics, and eighty-five for other achievements or contributions to the life of the school community. Most schools indicate, however, that their awards in the second and third categories are for group achievement, not individual. Only five schools do not make any such awards.

Carrots, then, there are in plenty to dangle in front of the nose of the most eager. But what of the stubborn laggards? They have fallen so far behind that the carrots are given up as lost anyway. So, in the traditional fashion of schoolmasters through the ages, we fall back on the whip. I speak metaphorically here, for although seventy-five schools in a hundred use corporal punishment, it is only as a last resort. (When it has to be used, the chosen instrument is nearly always the cane, though both strap and slipper get infrequent mention.) One headmaster, who admits to caning sometimes, says: 'I dislike it more than ever as a form of punishment.' Another says: 'I doubt its efficiency, and do not now use it.' He would be supported by Professor E. B. Castle, at one time headmaster of the Quaker boarding school at Leighton Park, Reading, who has written that his became an infinitely better school when he finally laid aside his cane.[1] It is interesting, and in my view encouraging, to find that in what is probably the toughest district of all, corporal punishment is not used.

Detention, either after school or during the dinner hour, is easily the most common form of punishment, being practised regularly in seventy-eight schools. Impositions of various kinds (quite frequently, and surprisingly, the old-fashioned 'lines') are given in thirty-five schools. The remaining means of enforcing discipline are, in rough order of frequency: various kinds of order or conduct marks;

1. *People in School* (Heinemann, 1953), p. 23.

extra work; daily report cards; exclusion from normal routine or privileges; letter to or interview with parents; fatigues or socially useful work, e.g. the collection of litter, to make amends for anti-social behaviour; and suspension from school. Four schools say that they have practically no official forms of punishment.

A striking feature is the extent to which schools deal with children (even in 'the last resort') on their own, rather than consulting the parents. As school becomes more obviously enjoyable and worthwhile to children, one hopes that temporary suspension, with the close collaboration of parents, will become the worst possible penalty, entirely replacing corporal punishment. For the rest, perhaps in twenty years' time the order of the other punishments will be reversed. We are moving, but, as in other matters, slowly.

Look at the eager faces in the early years of the primary schools; then look at the rows of reluctant fourteen-year-olds in so many secondary schools of all types. What have we done to them in the years between? The truest, healthiest incentive to learn lies within us and is spontaneous. Wrong ideas about what and how children should learn have made schoolmasters in the dark ages of education resort to the crude incentives of force. Less brutal but still damaging are many incentives practised today: rewards for the minority which are exclusive, carrying rejection for the unselected (e.g. prizes, prefect badges, comparative marks, ranking orders); and punishments which are no more than penalties, doing nothing to put the offender on a better path and help him to see the light.

Such incentives, whether rewards or punishments, act like purgatives on lazy bowels, and are just as harmful. For as the bowel comes to expect stimulation from outside and will not work without it, so the child in this competition-ridden world behaves likewise.

The twin emotions of envy and jealousy, says Angus Wilson, are 'abnormally in evidence in our schooldays; it is then that the competitive spirit, fostered by the closed hot-house atmosphere, twists and twines its liana grip round the lives of the young – a bracing preparation, it is said, for the jungle world to come'.[1]

Very few schools have rejected these external spurs. The lead has in fact been given by independent 'progressive' schools such as Summerhill and Dartington Hall, and this is one reason good enough in itself to make us beware of ever creating a purely State-controlled educational monolith. Now, tentatively at first but with growing boldness, a handful of maintained schools are beginning to follow. But it is still very much a minority movement.

Houses and tutorial groups

How useful are the house system and tutorial groups? The former exists in ninety-five per cent of the comprehensive schools, even (in attenuated form) in some of those whose basic organization is horizontal – i.e. lower, middle, and upper schools. Very occasionally the 'house' is an organization for games only. More frequently it extends to the social life of the school, and sometimes house groups are also classes for physical education, religious studies, crafts, and fine arts. Where house rooms or separate buildings are provided, the house is often an administrative centre too, with records, registers, reports, meals, cloakrooms, and many teams and clubs based on it.

There is no uniform pattern of house organization. A mixed school of 1,500 children may have five boys' houses and five girls' houses of 150 each, or it may have five mixed houses of 300 pupils each. It is difficult to see how the former arrangement, formally separating boys from girls in what is meant to be the kernel of a school's social life,

1. *Sunday Times*, 10 December 1961.

can be justified in a comprehensive coeducational community.

Within the house are tutorial groups. Each member of staff is attached to a house, and nearly all assistant teachers, apart from the housemaster or housemistress, have a group of some thirty children each put in their care. It may be a group of either boys or girls, or of both boys and girls, all of one age; or it may be a cross-section of the school's age range, eleven to eighteen. In either case the tutor usually remains with his charges throughout their school life, though where personal antipathy exists between tutor and pupil, as must occasionally happen, the latter is transferred to another group.

There are obvious attractions in the idea of breaking the large school down into smaller divisions. The picture of a personal tutor watching over the interests of each child, in close touch with his parents, collecting and assimilating information about him from other members of staff, guiding his pupil in the choice of courses and the many personal problems of school life, is a fine, idealistic one. There is no doubt that not only in schools of over 1,000, but in most schools of 500 or so too, care of this kind is needed. It would transform the effectiveness of our education. All honour, then, to those heads who are trying to make the vision a reality.

We must, however, recognize that at present the reality often falls a good way short of the aim. Some teachers are good personal tutors of this kind, many are not. Even when everybody is pressed into service, the tutorial groups are too big. Frequent changes of staff, common in all types of school, wreck the idea of a longstanding relationship slowly built up. Further, the base from which the tutors start is an artificial and often inadequate one. Some of their flock they will teach rarely or never; and although this does not matter so much if they share out-of-class interests such as games or music or drama, it is difficult to manufacture points of contact where some common interest does not already exist. That is why the interests of pupils in a small school (say 300) are often better served by the whole body of staff, perhaps fifteen teachers in all, acting in concert. Among these fifteen there is a real chance that natural affinity and interests will exist between each pupil and at least one of the teachers – but in addition every pupil will know all the staff, and they will all feel both a corporate and a personal responsibility for each of the 300.

It may be felt that the staff of a house could fill this role; but this brings us to the artificial character and limited scope of any house system in a day school. The house is peripheral to the core of a school's activity, the main reason for a school's existence: work. The heart of the school is the classroom. It is through the difficulties and satisfactions of working together that the most genuine and lasting personal relations are built up, and the house in a day school simply has not got this basis. Relatively little teaching is done in the mixed-ability house groups.

The more one tries to overcome this weakness by stressing the importance of the house, the more one may be increasing the difficulties. Take, for example, a housemaster who does quite a lot of administration. He may, as one housemaster has observed, know the bright twenty per cent very well, the most troublesome twenty per cent even better, but the remaining sixty per cent very little. Moreover, the longer pupils stay at school and concentrate increasingly on the subjects they like, the more their real allegiance is given to the teachers of those subjects. Where – as is not uncommon – housemasters are non-graduates and perhaps never teach the fifth or sixth forms, they sometimes find the older members of their house growing away from them. Unless the housemaster can make the same subtle change of attitude towards a sixth-former which is taken for granted in grammar schools, he will find himself rapidly estranged and resented.

Segregation in separate houses, too, in many cases has little appeal for the sixth-former. He has little in common with the majority of pupils in the house; his horizon is widening, and he wants to revel in the society of his contemporaries. Most of them will be taking different courses, and he may see all too little of them if he stays largely confined to the house community.

If we are to have houses, there would seem to be a strong case for confining them to the eleven-to-sixteen age group, or even (bearing Wandsworth's lower school in mind) the thirteen-to-sixteen group, and bringing all the sixth-formers together, with their own large commonroom and studies, at the top of the school. Apart from meeting their special needs, such a drawing together should have a unifying effect both symbolic and practical. Moreover it might then be possible to use only the really suitable members of staff as tutors. It would be interesting and informative if a school in Coventry, for example, with its strongly-developed house system, were to make special provision for the sixth form on these lines.

Wandsworth School in London – like Caludon Castle in Coventry – has a different combination of horizontal and vertical divisions: lower school eleven to thirteen (in the old grammar-school building but at the heart of the site) and houses thirteen to eighteen. By this means the gregarious younger boys get an ideal transition period between primary and full secondary education. They are not sealed off from the upper school, but are not thrown into it. There are informal contacts, and some teachers work in both lower and upper schools. Tutorial groups start at thirteen, and cover the adolescent stage when wise advice and sympathy from someone outside home are so often needed.

This pattern fits with that of the curriculum, with the foundation course to thirteen and biases developing beyond. It has the virtue of having evolved over many years. The tutorial group was begun by Raymond King, the now-retiring head, at Scarborough High School in 1926, and at Wandsworth (then a grammar school) in 1932. There is, indeed, a mellow quality about Wandsworth and its head which foreshadows what the normal English comprehensive school of the future will be like.

As Lenin and Stalin emphasized, theory without practice is sterile, practice without theory is blind. Principles must relate to empirical fact. For this reason my own preference, when faced with the need for smaller units within a large school, remains the horizontal division into lower and upper schools, with a break at fourteen.[1] An extra 'middle' division makes the whole thing too bitty, and moreover implies that basic general education, the 'foundation course', covers only two years instead of three. There is time enough to start specializing from fourteen onwards, particularly when the leaving age is raised to sixteen; and we must plan with that in mind.

Further, I believe that the natural choice as tutor for a group of day-school children is the form teacher, and that the form teacher should normally be the person who takes the class most often. Sometimes he may be able to move up the school with them a little way. Even during one year he is better placed than anyone else to fill the role of warden and guide described above. There are many teachers doing a competent job in these circumstances who find it impossible to forge a personal and group relationship out of little or nothing.

The boarding-school house is a substitute for the child's home. It is an acceptable substitute for a poor home, but a very moderate one for a good home. I am not yet con-

1. *Comprehensive Schools Today*, pp. 23-4.

vinced that its counterpart in a day school is necessary. Indeed, there are great dangers in schools attempting too much on their own. On the other hand, if the house system makes contact between school and home easier and more informal, and involves parents more closely in school affairs, it is well worth having. In one or two schools each house has its own parent-teacher association, which must assist this *rapport*.

All in all, despite the current popularity of the house system, one's verdict must still be 'not proven'. One head, who himself runs such a system, sums it up: 'I am uncertain whether this panders to fashion or is of real value.'

Social mixing

I have suggested that work groups are the most natural, most cohesive social units. If this is so, it explains why English comprehensive schools are on the horns of a dilemma, and why they are so keen to devise an alternative and parallel social system (houses with tutorial groups) which will bring pupils of all kinds of interest, background, and ability together. The accepted practice of 'streaming' children in groups of similar ability would otherwise mean that within one school there might develop cliques of clever children, gangs of backward ones. Certainly one might expect a tendency to drift apart, although this would be offset here and there by home friendships and special interests (e.g. games) which cut across the ability barrier.

The formation of very firm, exclusive circles based on common abilities and aptitudes is to some extent thwarted by the practice of 'setting', which means rearranging the children's classes according to their ability in different subjects. This in turn, however, involves a loss. There is such a thing as group personality, a highly important factor in any teaching situation; and it is difficult for such a personality to evolve if the stability of the group is constantly being upset by changes of membership. I recall the wise words of a former headmistress of Douglas Girls' High School: 'We try not to be too restless.'

Small sample studies recently conducted by Mr G. V. Pape suggest that in a comprehensive school with a strongly-developed house system, girls 'do not stick to their formmates. They are just as likely to be found mixing with other members of their house who are in different forms.' On the other hand, he found that in a grammar school without such a system they 'separate themselves off within the school, both inside the classroom and outside, into still finer ability groupings corresponding to the graded forms'.[1] His study does not claim to amount to anything like a final judgement, but it suggests that the house system is helping to counteract the segregationist influence of streaming.

Social activities

There is a luxuriant growth of clubs, teams, excursions, and societies of all kinds in almost all the comprehensive schools. One Yorkshire school, not exceptional, has nineteen different school societies, and twelve games and athletic clubs. It organizes many visits abroad, in Britain, and in its own locality. Wales, as one might expect, is particularly strong in music; for example, a school of 900 has a full orchestra with string, brass, and wood sections, and another's operatic society is particularly outstanding. Several schools have careers conventions each session, with visiting speakers.

At the Yorkshire school mentioned, not only are upper-school pupils invited to all parent-teacher association socials and dances, but the upper school runs its own dances and various other activities. Another northern

Monday		Tuesday		Wednesday		Thursday		Friday	
Activity	Open to	Activity	Open to	Activity	Open to	Activity	Open to	Activity	Open to
Chess Club (L)	All years	Chess Club	All	Geography Club (L)	All	History Club (L)	Years 1–3	Swimming Club (before school)	All
Christian Fellowship (L)	Years 1 and 2	Recorders (L)	Year 1	Christian Fellowship (L) P.E. Club	Year 1 and 2	Boat building	Year 3 and up	French plays (L)	Year 2
Recorders (L)	Years 1–4	Art Club (L)	All	Boat building	All	Handicraft Club	All	Recorders (L)	Year 1
Handicraft Club	All	Drama Club	Year 3 and up	Choir (School)	Year 3 and up	Past and Present Tennis Club	Seniors	Fencing	Year 2 and up
Debate and Discussion	Year 3 and up	Choir	Year 1	Handicraft Club	All	Science Models	Years 4 and 5	Piano Class	All
P.E. Training Club	All	Badminton	All	Fencing	Year 2 and up	Drama Club – Speech for Duke of Edinburgh	All		
Stamp	All	First Aid, Duke of Edinburgh	Boys	Games Club – girls	Years 1 and 2		Year 4		
Biology	Year 3 and up	Swimming Club	Year 2 and up	Drama Club	Years 1 and 2	Art Club	Year 1		
Orchestra	All	Dress Design Club	Year 3 and up	Dress Design	Year 3 and up				
Violin Classes	All			Duke of Edinburgh	Year 4 and up				
Brass band	All								
Duke of Edinburgh	Over 14								
Photography	All								

All clubs are at the end of afternoon school unless marked (L), when they are held at lunch time. An all-houses advisory session for pupils and parents is held from 4 to 5 p.m. every day. Recreational evenings (one house per evening) and parents' interviews (Year 3 and up) are held from 5.30 to 7.30 p.m. every evening except Friday. Reproduced from *London Comprehensive Schools*, p. 30.

school has no traditional Speech Day, but an Open Day with an exhibition of work to parents and public; this exhibition is visited by over 3,000 people. But social activities are by no means all concerned solely with the interests and welfare of the public. Service to the community is often stressed. For example, in World Refugee Year a rural school of 550 pupils adopted a refugee family and raised £450 to help to buy land and build a home for them.

I have mentioned but a few from the enormous range of activities. The table on page 129 gives an idea of what goes on every week at one London comprehensive school.

This rich diversity of out-of-class activities is wholly admirable. It is a testimony to the devoted work of hundreds of teachers. A big school can of course offer a greater variety of such pursuits. There is perhaps one danger — that the pursuit of excellence may cause some keen teachers, who can pick and choose from a large number of pupils, to set the standard of performance (in music, for example) so high that only the gifted benefit. The mass of ordinary people, though liking music and at first willing to try, may then feel that it is not for them. Public performances have their value, but also their limitations.

English comprehensive schools, then, are vigorous societies. There is efficient planning, administration, and teaching of an orthodox kind. The children are graded on ability in the subjects which lead to examinations, but an attempt is made, not unsuccessfully, to offset the possibly harmful social effects of this grading by the development of houses with tutorial groups of completely mixed ability. Within this system the children have opportunity to move upwards — though streaming and setting probably widen the gaps and harden the divisions as time passes. Out of class there is every facility for recreation and cultural pursuits. These schools compare favourably with other kinds of secondary schools in the range and quality of the education they provide.

It is possible to make such comparison fairly because fundamentally the comprehensive schools are trying to do the same job as the older schools, but to do it better. They still proceed by selection – though it is smoother, continuous, more efficient selection. They keep the pupils busy and happy developing their special interests and talents in all manner of ways – but it is very largely an adult-inspired programme, relying on the voluntary efforts of many teachers for its success.

There is, however, still something missing, which must be found and introduced if these schools are to grow to full stature. We cannot settle for a school which simply cuts out the worst inefficiencies of its grammar and 'modern' predecessors and prepares its pupils more effectively for the old social pyramid. Such a school can quickly become a streaming, streamlined machine, grooming everyone for an appropriate place in the meritocracy of 1984 and after.

At present too many comprehensive schools seem set to speed the coming of that 'brave new world'. If it were so, democrats might well fear and oppose them much more than do the diehard representatives of social privilege, the stupid leaders full of their own imagined superiority who are the crusty shell of every political party. Such schools ought to be, and perhaps by 1970 they will be, the darlings of *Crossbow*.

But they are not the whole picture. Here and there new men and women are rising who not only question old assumptions, but whose practice is proving how empty are the old beliefs. Such people may yet establish to England's satisfaction that democracy in schools is not only possible but necessary. And the men of the middle way are essential too. Their contribution to peaceful evolution must never be underrated. For, avoiding controversy and winning acceptance in the terms best understood today, they yet look from the old to the new with calm assurance and open minds. That is why, though I could never be satisfied that these schools should remain as they are, I am not unhopeful of the future.

The school in society

As a concept the comprehensive school is above all a school for the community. How far is it fulfilling this idea?

The picture is a very uneven one. Many schools are still withdrawn, after the rather stilted, aloof English custom. As we have seen, many teachers tend to think of the school as a tight professional preserve which is their concern and nobody else's. They even manage to sell this to parents. Parents' Associations, like football supporters' clubs, often accept as their aim 'assistance without interference'.

There is always a borderland where the special interests and qualifications of parent and teacher overlap. Should school uniform be compulsory or even 'expected'? What restrictions on children's dress, hair style, adornments, are reasonable? Who is the final authority on conduct out of school? Should corporal punishment be used, and if so, in what circumstances? Ought a headmaster to have the power to forbid a seventeen-year-old cricketer to play for a league side on Saturday afternoon, and to compel him instead to turn out for the school in a game much inferior in standard?

Where teachers and parents, with conviction, hold opposing views on such matters, clashes are bound to arise. In England we and the courts back the teachers almost automatically. A teacher has to do something manifestly wrong before he is condemned. We *want* him to be thought right. Teachers too easily forget this when they complain of 'inferior status'. To what other classes of the community does this spontaneous support apply? By contrast, a solicitor or an accountant is given much less mercy if his conduct is brought into question. Can it be that teachers as a body have an uneasy conscience because they do not and of course cannot live up to the high standards which their former pupils want them to have?

The idol always has feet of clay. Goldsmith's village schoolmaster was, doubtless, something of an impostor.

> And still they gazed, and still the wonder grew
> That one small head could carry all he knew.

Children invest parents and teachers with godlike qualities. With maturity comes disillusion. The great test of adults is how far they can change worship into understanding love rather than hurt disappointment. For this reason it is dangerous, and a sign of inner weakness, for adults to seek to maintain their prestige by extending the authoritarian role unchanged from infants to adolescents. The adolescents of today are the parents of tomorrow.

In America the parent has much more say, both in the social education of the child and in his choice of curriculum. 'When the chips are down,' a Canadian headmaster tells me, 'it's the parent and pupil who decide.'

Here, in the relations between school and local society, is a wonderful opportunity for adult education. Parents and teachers have one binding interest, the child's welfare. Because most adults become parents at some time or other, they are nearly all approachable through a medium which concerns them intimately. I wish that the Workers' Educational Association, instead of providing quite so many classes in philosophy, psychology, art, and music, and becoming a purveyor of middle-class 'culture' to would-be intellectuals, could take a leading role in this field. It is possibly the only way of involving the working class *as a whole* in the sort of education which they find meaningful. Through the intimate interweaving of school and local society, the promotion of a classless, communal culture is a practical possibility: not, I repeat, a flat, common culture, but one whose basic values (such as truth, tolerance, courage, justice, and beauty) would be accepted by all, one leading to lives rich in purpose and variety.

The W.E.A. has always had sane far-sighted views on schools, but it has with great propriety spoken from the outside and has usually confined itself to ideas about the framework of the system. It has in fact tacitly accepted the prickly insistence of the teaching profession that what happens in schools, and often in the relations between school and neighbourhood, is exclusively their concern. As one who grew up in the W.E.A., I am deeply disturbed that it should now be on the defensive, fighting for its continued existence, undermined by its growing middle-class, intellectual, anti-political membership.

If the job it was meant to do were in fact completed, there would be no more to be said. But it has scarcely begun. I believe that the W.E.A., with its great record of social and political (non-party political) wisdom, is far better equipped to do this job than the middle-class pressure groups called 'Associations for the advancement of State education' which have sprung up to fill the vacuum, useful though these may be in the short term.

But the W.E.A. cannot act alone. The churches, too, like other voluntary bodies, should be involved. Above all, the teachers' associations must throw aside the shield of reserve behind which they shelter from the honest scrutiny of their fellows. They must stop sitting on the fence on matters of clear principle like the eleven-plus examination because they fear for the vested interests of their members. If they are to earn the regard of the community, as they certainly yearn for it, they should today be actively promoting the most lively and searching discussion around their schools concerning what goes on inside them.

The first English comprehensive schools are, on the whole, still too self-contained. They should not be blamed for this. Here, as in so much else, they have inherited a long tradition. Moreover they have been so preoccupied with winning acceptance on current standards – examination results, conduct, cultural activities, and so on – that they have had little time, even when the inclination is there, to venture beyond the frontier of contemporary educational practice. Sometimes local political circumstances have been such that it would have been foolish to do so. The art of timing is at the heart of success in men's affairs, and the climate has not always favoured bold enterprises.

It is equally true, however, that in human life we cannot mark time for long. If we do not go forward, we slip back. When we cease to grow, we start to die. The time is becoming overdue for a major advance in the relations between our community schools and the community itself.

In 1961–2 I found that only forty-eight out of a hundred schools had a parent-teacher association or similar body. It was felt by many heads of schools without such associations that they are liable to be dominated by middle-class parents: 'The parents I want to see are those who would never come – parents of the C stream.' They prefer meetings specially and separately arranged for parents of particular classes, first year, second year, and so on.

But although there is much to be said for such special meetings, it is not usually possible for parents at such gatherings to do more than discuss their own children's progress with the teachers. There is little or no opportunity to discover and discuss common ground with other parents – and one has an uncomfortable feeling that many heads do not want this. Nor is the absence of C-stream parents from parent-teacher associations a good reason for depriving other parents of the chance to discuss educational principles as applied in their children's school. It may be a reason for questioning the existence of categories like 'C stream' at all. It may indicate the need for teachers to go out and get to know absentee parents in their own homes and bring them in – but not to close down channels of contact for everyone.

The difficulty of parents getting to and from school in the evenings is a big obstacle in rural areas. But, as we have seen, that very difficulty inspired Henry Morris to set up his village colleges in Cambridgeshire. The village college idea is a two-way current. People pour in to the centre, teachers go out to the villages and hamlets. The outgoing is essential. It is the part obviously missing so far from the work of comprehensive schools, though in Leicestershire 'modern' and junior comprehensive schools are being made bases for local community colleges on Cambridgeshire lines.

In eighty out of a hundred schools, however, the buildings are used by people of the neighbourhood at evenings or week-ends for social and/or educational activities. Two schools have the local branch of the county library on the premises. On one Merseyside estate, clubs meet regularly in the evenings.

The big deficiency, which is not peculiar to comprehensive schools, is the lack of direct contact by teachers with their pupils' homes. American schools have their guidance departments of specially qualified people. We need them too; but it is essential that when they come they shall aid teachers to do a bigger and wider job, including welfare, not allow them to withdraw still more into specialist teaching alone.

The most valuable contacts are often those made informally by people sharing in local activities. It happens

easily enough in country towns; it *ought* to happen, and
would be still more valuable, in the cities and on housing
estates. But this demands that teachers shall live in the district served by the school, and a great many prefer to 'get
away from it all' by living elsewhere. One sympathizes, for
they are often tired from overwork. But could the boarding school survive if its staff went as far away as possible
as soon as formal schooling ended? Could the priest feel
that he earned even his meagre salary if he merely conducted the services, the church council and vestry meetings,
and the Sunday School outing?

I have criticized much in English schools and teachers.
But they have their strengths as well as their weaknesses,
and the former must not be swept away with the latter.
One of their most valuable features in the past has been the
pastoral care bestowed on their pupils. Bigger schools, a
shortage of teachers, improved transport, the greater
mobility of society – all these have gone far to destroy it.
Perhaps this is the most important reason why boarding
schools are becoming more popular; they are the best substitute we have for the real thing. There is no doubt in my
mind that it is in the neighbourhood school, in which
children, parents, teachers, and others meet and mingle,
that the fullest preparation for a rich, purposeful life in a
democratic society can be gained.

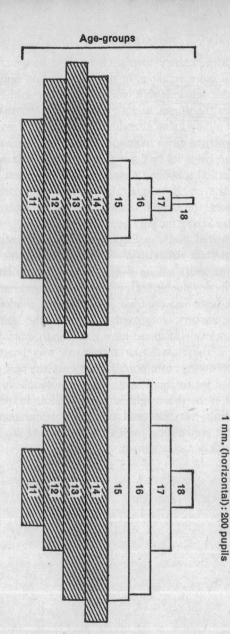

Age-groups

I. ALL L.E.A. SECONDARY SCHOOLS
(England and Wales: January 1961)
1 mm. (horizontal): 10,000 pupils

11 12 13 14 15 16 17 18

II. ALL RECOGNIZED INDEPENDENT
SECONDARY SCHOOLS
(England and Wales: January 1961)
1 mm. (horizontal): 200 pupils

11 12 13 14 15 16 17 18

4. Different Forms of Comprehensive Education

THERE is widespread agreement that segregation at eleven-plus ought to be abolished. There is also, however, a good deal of reluctance to accept the ordinary comprehensive secondary school (eleven to eighteen) as the alternative. Before we proceed to consider what may be more generally acceptable solutions, it is necessary to summarize the main objections to the latter. They turn on the question of efficiency at sixth-form level.

In a nutshell, the argument is this: (1) a comprehensive school needs to have a sixth form of at least 120 pupils if it is to meet modern requirements; (2) on average it takes a comprehensive school of 1,500 pupils aged eleven to eighteen to produce a sixth form of this size (when the leaving age is raised to sixteen, probably 1,000 pupils); (3) there are educational objections to such large schools; (4) even if these objections are thought invalid, it is certain that large schools sufficient in number to house all children of secondary age cannot be provided for many, many years – yet the need to reform the segregated school system is urgent.

Let me take these points in turn.

1. I have already argued that a sixth-form class of optimum size numbers perhaps eight to twelve pupils. This ensures reasonable economy in the use of highly-qualified teachers, who are all too scarce. It also promotes educational efficiency; the group is small enough to allow the teacher to attend properly to each pupil, big enough to encourage lively discussion.

A school catering for all sorts and conditions of students should offer twenty subjects or more at advanced level, if it is to do the job properly. Each of the following departments will itself need to provide two, three, or perhaps four subjects: modern languages, classics, science, mathematics, engineering, commercial subjects, housecraft, heavy crafts, and the fine arts. Since the sixth form is a stage of education covering at least two and often three years, a fully developed comprehensive school may expect to have at least fifty sixth-form classes. Each pupil will be a member of perhaps four of these. If the normal size of these classes is around ten pupils, as I have suggested it should be, a sixth form of 120 or more becomes necessary to justify staffing and equipment on a really efficient scale.

Dr Richard Lynn has shown that schools with large sixth forms do distinctly better *per pupil*, in work for the advanced level of GCE, than schools with small sixth forms.[1] He found, first, that girls' grammar schools in London, with much smaller sixth forms, got only half the distinctions per hundred pupils that the boys' schools did. This can hardly be due to a different level of intelligence between boys and girls. Secondly, he found that while the large boys' grammar schools got only eight per cent more passes at ordinary level than the smaller boys' grammar schools, two years later, at advanced level, they got a hundred per cent more distinctions per hundred candidates. This must be due to superior sixth-form education in the larger schools.

In open scholarships to Oxford and Cambridge this tendency is even more pronounced. Certainly the leading schools in the Oxbridge scholarship-league tables over the years have been such schools as Manchester G.S. (550 in the sixth form: 32 open awards in 1960–1); Dulwich (477:30); Winchester (330:25); St Paul's (409:22); and Marlborough (500:17).[2]

1. *British Journal of Sociology*, June 1959, pp. 129–36.
2. *The Times Educational Supplement*, 28 July 1961: G. D. N. Worswick, 'Men's Awards at Oxbridge, 1960–1'.

2. If we could have an average local secondary school the size of whose age-groups was in proportion to the Ministry of Education's aggregated figures for all the maintained secondary schools in England and Wales in 1961, it would need to total 3,000 pupils aged eleven to eighteen in order to produce 120 of that number in the sixth form. Contrast this with a leading independent school such as Rugby, which has a thirteen-to-eighteen age-range, and where about half of the 700 boys do sixth-form work. The picture in recognized independent secondary schools as a whole is similar, as the diagram on page 138 shows.

Numbers at the top of the independent 'public' school justify the provision of well-qualified staff and ample equipment. There is no extravagance, for both are fully used. Yet because the proportion of older pupils is high, total numbers need not be great.

Those comprehensive schools which have been established for some years, however, are keeping at school after fifteen up to twice as many pupils as the average for the country as a whole. We may therefore accept that schools of 1,500, not 3,000, will probably meet the requirement of 120 in the sixth form. When compulsory schooling is extended to sixteen the picture will be transformed. Comprehensive schools of no more than 1,000 pupils aged eleven to eighteen may reasonably expect to have 120 or more engaged in sixth, seventh, and eighth year courses.

3. The educational objections to very big schools are as follows.

First, they tend to be run on a hierarchical basis. The ordinary class teacher may find himself far removed from the centre of effective discussion and decision. In the small school he counts for a lot, in the big school for much less. Offsetting this, however, he is likely to find a bigger staff more stimulating. Where there are people with a great variety of interests and qualifications, the environment of the staffroom is likely to be rich and diverse, never mean and narrow.

Secondly, in a big school the intimacy necessary for the deeprooted growth of a community is much more difficult to achieve. In the small school, whether you happen to teach a child or not, you and he still know each other quite well. Your responsibility for him, his responsibility to you, are taken for granted by both. In the outsize school, to note good or bad behaviour you may need your note-book, like a policeman, to get the boy's name and class. A chit is called for to inform his tutor, if in a busy day it seems worth-while going to those lengths. A hundred yards outside the school, pupil and teacher may each be to the other no more than a vaguely familiar face, the most casual of acquaintances.[1]

A teacher commented to me on his own big school's carol festival: 'As many as 300 children take part; several choirs are involved, soloists, the school orchestra. But one comes to long for smaller numbers on the platform, a more intimate atmosphere, less tramping about of pupils between carols.'

Objections of this kind apply to all big schools, of course, whatever the type. They find expression in stories such as the doubtless apocryphal one of two boys who were taking a scholarship at Oxford: 'Which school do you come from ?' 'Manchester Grammar School.' 'So do I.'

Finally, the average child. We need not worry here about the bright, the dull, the delinquent, the unusual of any sort

1. The former head of a comprehensive school, Mrs H. R. Chet-wynd, gives a different view: 'By keeping records on paper and not in our heads, the method suggested as a better alternative, we place our knowledge based on personal contact at the disposal of all other interested colleagues who wish to share our understanding of the child.' (*Comprehensive School*, Routledge and Kegan Paul, 1960, pp. 101–2).

– they always win attention. It is the ordinary boy who needs to feel that he counts – not for anything special that he can do (he often cannot do anything special), but simply for himself. In spite of the division of big schools into smaller social units such as houses and tutorial groups, many fear that he will be overlooked. Comprehensive school teachers certainly try to prevent this, but I have found them divided on the extent to which they are successful.

4. The educational objections are very largely matters of opinion. Some will dismiss them, and they may be right in doing so. We must nevertheless face the fact that out of 5,847 secondary schools in England and Wales in 1961, only 127 provided for more than 1,000 pupils; and no more than 404 schools (including those 127) took more than 800 pupils. At the other extreme, 2,285 secondary schools had fewer than 400 pupils.

Many of our schools occupy post-war buildings which cannot conceivably be scrapped. The capital investment required to replace them by schools for over 1,000 pupils would be enormous. New spacious sites would often be impossible to find. The whole programme would take many years to implement – too many. If one believes that segregation at eleven is harmful, such delay in starting the necessary reforms becomes intolerable. Another solution must be found.

Two-tier secondary education

There is such an alternative to the very large school. It has been canvassed in this country ever since 1944 in various forms, and it has its precedents abroad, particularly in North America.

Immediately following the 1944 Act it was obvious to a small minority of people that the drawbacks of selection at eleven on the one hand and huge comprehensive schools on the other could be resolved – and, moreover, quickly and economically resolved – by putting existing small and medium-sized schools end-on to provide secondary education in two stages.[1] In 1954 Croydon's education officials made a powerful case for combining all the borough's sixth forms in a 'junior college'. Early proposals for such reform, however, foundered on two rocks: the slightness of statistical evidence against selection at eleven, and the reluctance of grammar-school and comprehensive-school teachers to lose their older pupils to a separate institution.

From about 1953 onwards, however, parents' dissatisfaction with eleven-plus selection began to receive weighty backing from the researches of scholars and from facts given in the official report on *Early Leaving* (1954). This report showed that of the twenty children in every hundred picked for grammar schools at the age of eleven, barely nine reached the normal grammar-school target of five or more passes at the ordinary level of GCE, or an equivalent standard. Indeed, of those who were in the top third of the eleven-plus pass lists, fewer than two out of three were successful by this criterion. On the other hand, late transfers to the grammar school of those who had originally failed at eleven came out slightly better than the whole group of eleven-plus successes.

By the mid-fifties the number of pupils staying longer at school had increased to such an extent that a two-tier system no longer necessarily involved the decapitation of the grammar schools; all but the tiniest could become schools for higher secondary education only. Most 'modern' schools, for their part, had developed well enough to contemplate tackling the early years of secondary education for all pupils.

1. cf. *Education*, 18 and 25 February 1949, R. Pedley, 'County College and Sixth Form', and Labour Party, *Challenge to Britain*, 1953.

This new evidence[1] aroused the interest of administrators at both national and local levels. For example, in May 1955 I was invited to put to the Midland branch of the Association of Education Officers the case for the two-tier system as it might apply in this country. At a meeting with the Minister of Education and senior officials at the Ministry in the following year (1956) I suggested an interim scheme whereby all children should go direct from primary to the existing 'modern' schools, which would thus become junior comprehensive schools, and spend at least three years there. At the age of fourteen, all who wished to go to the grammar schools would do so without examination, provided their parents agreed to keep them there for at least two years. The others would complete their education in the junior comprehensive school.

The advantages of this modified plan were as follows:

1. The secondary schooling of all children who stayed in the converted 'modern' schools would be unbroken.

2. Those going to the grammar school at fourteen would have two years before taking the GCE, like most entrants to 'public' schools.

3. It was likely to be more acceptable to grammar school teachers than would be the transfer of all children at fourteen or fifteen. Though they would have to start coping with a much wider range of ability, at least there was a precedent for that in the pre-war days of fee-payers. Their recruits would at any rate be willing – or at worst would be the unwilling children of willing parents, who could be relied upon to support the school.

4. A promise to keep children at grammar schools for at

1. cf. R. Pedley, 'Comprehensive Education: a non-party solution' (*Schoolmaster*, 8 April 1955), 'The Way Ahead' (*Schoolmaster*, 23 November 1956), and *Comprehensive Education: a new approach* (Gollancz, 1956).

least two years, though it could not be enforced, would ensure that parents did not lightly choose a grammar-school education for one year only, for the sake of status.

In making these proposals I was aware of some obvious deficiencies. The two-year undertaking would have the effect of discouraging poor parents, or those parents, usually working-class, who do not readily see the value of higher education and would not commit themselves for two years ahead. The new style 'grammar school' would be neither a selective school for academic pupils nor a proper senior comprehensive school. It would in fact be much more like the local grammar school of pre-war days, except that ability to pay a modest fee for day pupils would now be replaced by ability and willingness to keep the child longer at school. Again, the creation of a 'rump' of pupils in the last year of the converted 'modern' school did not look like a permanently satisfactory solution. They would be the pupils who had decided that they wished to leave school as soon as possible, and had nothing more to work for, who seemed likely to be the less able and less well-behaved boys and girls, too.

The plan was envisaged only as an interim measure. Its great virtue seemed that it offered a practical way, under existing conditions, of doing away with the eleven-plus examination and enforced segregation of children there-after. It would be a step on the way to a still better system.

The experiment in Leicestershire

In the following year (1957) Leicestershire decided to adopt in two areas, Wigston and Hinckley, a plan very similar to that described above. The main difference lay in the county's decision to accelerate the progress of very bright children from the primary school to the sixth form by promoting these 'flyers' (roughly eight to ten per cent of a whole age-group) from primary to the new junior high school at the age of ten, and from the junior high school to the senior grammar school at thirteen. By this means, such bright pupils would be able to take GCE (ordinary level) at fifteen and gain an extra year in the sixth form. This early transfer of 'flyers' necessarily involves the movement of some children from primary to secondary education below the legal minimum age of ten years six months. It is, however, commonly practised by other local education authorities, and the Ministry turns a blind eye on it.

The scheme was begun in Leicestershire in a modified way. Free transfer from 'modern' to grammar school at fourteen for all who wished it was introduced at once, and this ensured a welcome from many worried and disappointed parents; but for the first two years at Wigston, and the first three at Hinckley, problems of accommodation made it necessary for the authority to continue to select the top twelve and a half per cent for direct transfer from primary to grammar schools at the age of eleven. This has now ceased – and with it, the eleven-plus examination. Indeed, the reorganized districts of Leicestershire are the only areas in England (not Wales) where the eleven-plus has been abolished. All children, whether promoted normally at eleven-plus or early at ten-plus, spend three years in the converted 'modern' school, now termed 'high school'. At fourteen (thirteen for the exceptional cases) parents decide whether they wish their child to go to the grammar school for at least two more years. If so, they are asked to sign a statement to this effect.

The scheme has since been launched in a third district, Birstall, and is being extended to other parts of the county as soon as possible.

It is, as yet, too soon to give any final answer on the merits and demerits of this particular version of the two-tier plan, for not until 1964 at Wigston (1965 at Hinckley) shall we have even the ordinary level GCE results from the first full age-group to go through the new system. It will be 1966 (1967) before their advanced-level results, on which the products of grammar schools are increasingly being judged, will be known. Nevertheless some conclusions can be drawn, some pointers observed.

1. The lightening of eleven-plus pressure on the local junior schools, just as in areas served by orthodox comprehensive schools, has been marked. These schools have been freed to experiment with unstreamed classes and with fresh approaches to the teaching of mathematics, French, and other subjects. It would be partisan, however, to assume that this wave of progress wholly results from the ending of eleven-plus. Rather are such ideas part of the general educational climate of Leicester; and a lead in these matters has long come from certain junior schools in the city of Leicester, which retains the eleven-plus examination.

2. Probably the main benefit has been the transformation of the former 'modern' schools. For the first time since 1944 they have a place in the sun, as an essential link in a comprehensive chain. Extension of their work to cover the early years of a grammar-school course has required the appointment of teachers of such subjects as Latin, French, and the physical sciences, and a filling out of the work previously done in established subjects like mathematics. Generous financial provision for heads of departments and posts of special responsibility gives material satisfaction. Extra buildings and equipment have been provided. It is important to note, too, that the Minister has raised no objection to the provision of new schools to fit into this plan, although his approval is required for all new schools.

How good is the teaching of the bright children in these junior high schools? This is a question which to some extent will always be a matter of opinion. Good, bad, or indifferent examination results, when they emerge, will not afford a clear answer, for they will be affected both by later teaching in the grammar school and by the effect on children of transfer itself.

My own view is that the junior high-school teachers have fully justified the confidence of the plan's advocates. Their work has been devoted and effective. They, together with many teachers in 'modern' schools which are already running GCE courses, are proving themselves fully capable of teaching children of all kinds of ability up to the age, not merely of fourteen, but sixteen.

However, although the morale of the former 'modern' (now junior high) schools has been vastly strengthened, their internal organization is still orthodox. Here children are streamed, on the recommendation of the junior-school teachers, into A, B, and C streams, though with a six-form-entry school (a common size) there may be two parallel forms in each stream. Class-ranking orders are usually given to indicate children's relative progress, though there is not the fierce pressure created by the weekly or monthly results so familiar in many grammar schools. There are prefects, prizes, houses (not in separate buildings), and school uniforms. In their social organization these schools are unremarkable English secondary schools; and the same applies to their curricula and teaching methods.

We have noticed the arrangement which permits the brightest children to be promoted from primary to secondary school a year in advance. Intended to enable them to enter the sixth form at fifteen and spend three years there, it nevertheless seems to contradict the general philosophy behind the scheme. Though intellectually the equal of children a year older, with whom they are placed, 'flyers' are more immature physically and socially. Grammar-school sixth-form teachers sometimes find that such early arrivals are too immature to understand, say, political motives and social causation in history, or certain kinds of poetry and other literature. Quicksilver intelligence may easily swing adrift if it is not related in a balanced way to the development of an adolescent's whole personality. Such factors may have caused the proportion of children who are promoted early to be reduced to five per cent, and experience may well suggest further revision of the practice.

The main problems centre on two things: provision for the fourth-year remnant who do not choose to go to the senior grammar school at fourteen, and relations between senior grammar school and junior high school.

As was foreseen from the start, the former is a problem, though not a disabling one. It is one of the snags which are inseparable from interim solutions. On the whole these children are below the average in ability and see little purpose in a final year's schooling. As prefects they cannot be expected to offer the leadership and example, or exercise the control, that would be present in comprehensive schools going up to sixteen or eighteen. Courses with a modest bias towards practical, commercial, or technical subjects have been devised, and at Hinckley some of their teaching has been given, for a time, in the nearby college of further education; but so far the high schools would not claim to have found any magic key to these pupils' interests. External examinations are not taken in some of the high schools, though others take the examinations of the College of Preceptors or similar bodies. Would a local certificate help, modelled on the same lines as that which is so successful at Keighley, for example?

On the other hand it must be realized that the new scheme did not create this problem of the fourth-year leaver. It existed in the 'modern' school. Tragically, it exists in the fourth year C and D streams of not a few grammar schools, where neglected boys of no mean ability are sometimes turned into resentful rebels. The new order has largely smoothed away that resentful element from the junior high schools. Indeed, because their abler fellows have moved on to the grammar school, those who remain enjoy a status and the chance to exercise responsibility which in the ordinary way would not have been theirs.

When the leaving age is raised to sixteen, it will not be desirable to have a two-year rump of this kind. It may be necessary either to move everyone on to the senior grammar school at fourteen or to allow the junior high school to hold them to fifteen or sixteen and the ordinary level examinations of GCE. In either case these pupils will no longer feel that they have opted out of education, as they do now. Such a change would be particularly good for the handful of able children whose parents now refuse to let them go forward, and who may feel frustrated during the final year.

It will help to overcome the difference in opportunity created under the present optional system by parents' different social background. The Wigston area is largely professional and middle class; in 1961-2, fifty-six per cent of its fourteen-year-old children were in the senior grammar school and therefore going to stay at school till sixteen. Hinckley is largely industrial and working-class; in the same year only thirty-six per cent of its fourteen-year-old children were in that category. We have seen that orthodox comprehensive schools commonly keep from half to two-thirds of their pupils to the age of sixteen. A further indication of the difficulties of such an optional scheme in a working-class area is the fact that at Hinckley fewer girls than boys tend to go to the grammar school. Many parents still think that extended education for girls is a waste of time and money.

It seems that in Leicestershire more working-class parents ought to be choosing higher secondary education for their children. Detailed changes, like having the same basic uniform and so cutting out expense on transfer at fourteen, would help. But the main need is either general transfer at fourteen or the extension of the junior high schools into true high schools (eleven-to-sixteen) taking GCE and other examinations.

The relating of the curricula and particular syllabuses of the junior high and senior grammar schools is obviously important. Meetings of subject-teachers are held, and informal contact is of course always possible. In practice the success of these consultations and the degree of cooperation achieved naturally vary. To some extent there is a built-in conflict of interests. The junior-high-school teacher has no examination worries and is naturally inclined to spread himself, to move towards a broad education which seems desirable in itself. He is in the same position as the junior-school teacher freed from the cloud of the eleven-plus, and he must be expected to react in the same way. The senior-grammar-school teacher, on the other hand, sees the hurdle of GCE examinations only two years ahead of his new recruits. He is anxious that they shall get a flying start and be well grounded in what he considers the essentials of his subject. The change of school and teachers may itself slow up progress for a time, until everyone gets adjusted. He cannot afford further delays. It is clear that a certain similarity of views and harmony of personalities between the responsible teachers of the different subjects is very desirable, and that its absence can be a real drawback.

Yet even in the normal school system, the segregation of each teacher from others doing the same job is a grave weakness. It is possible for a man or woman to spend forty years in a classroom – perhaps the same classroom – without seeing another teacher teach, or even exchanging facts and ideas about content and methods. It is a great virtue of the two-tier plan that teachers in different schools are brought together to discuss and learn from one another's approaches. The task is really like that of a relay team whose success depends on passing the baton smoothly and well. It is an exercise in cooperation and coordination.

3. Finally, the senior grammar schools. Whereas reorganization for the 'modern' (junior-high) school has brought an obvious rise in status, many grammar-school teachers – though by no means all – regard it as bringing to them a fall in status. Some wish they could have the brightest children earlier; others may resent being asked to teach slow learners 'who should not be in a grammar school at all'.

The most impressive feature of the senior grammar school is its comprehensive provision for the pupils' various needs. All the normal grammar-school subjects, together with practical courses and the arts, are available. Courses for backward children, whose parents want them to continue schooling beyond fifteen, have been introduced and suitable teachers appointed. Both Wigston (1,100 pupils) and Hinckley (770) are too big at present, but a new senior grammar school at Oadby will soon reduce the load on the former.

At Wigston well over 450 pupils now enter the school each year, an influx greater than that at Kidbrooke or Crown Woods in London, Great Barr or Sheldon Heath in Birmingham. Since most pupils will be there for only two years, it is extremely difficult for the teachers to get to know them really well. The only external examination at present taken is the GCE. This means that the pupils who are not capable of taking GCE successfully may feel disappointed and frustrated. The proposed new Certificate of Secondary Education will doubtless fill the gap.

Pupils who stay for a sixth form course naturally feel that they count for more. Even here, however, classes in some popular subjects such as English and mathematics may rise to an excessive size for sixth-form work. I have severely criticized the tiny sixth-form class of one or two pupils. The class of twenty is at the other extreme at this stage. It makes very difficult the searching individual contact between teacher and pupil which is the essence of Crowther's 'intellectual discipleship'. The burden of marking may also be alarmingly heavy, unless the number of teaching periods can be greatly reduced.

Pupils entering senior grammar schools are streamed on the recommendation of the junior high schools. Backward children are taken by a teacher specially qualified for remedial work. The curriculum available is very wide, indeed comprehensive in scope, and the subject combinations are flexible. For example, a girl may commonly take English, French, art, and needlework in the sixth form; and there is no thought that any subject is superior to another.

Socially, the senior grammar schools are as orthodox as the junior high schools. School societies and the house system are no more significant than in most other grammar schools. A tutorial system, such as has been so carefully worked out in the orthodox comprehensive schools, could perhaps be developed with advantage. The wearing of school uniform is required. On the other hand there is a friendly atmosphere, at once relaxed and responsible, which better fits the concept of a more adult and democratic community.

The retention of the description 'grammar school' has led to some misunderstanding by both teachers and parents. To the historian it is justified, because many grammar schools were originally free to all local boys, and up to 1944 they catered for a wide range of ability, with a mixture of fee-payers and scholarship pupils. But since that time grammar schools have come to be thought of as schools for the academic élite. Many grammar-school teachers, aided and abetted by Lord James, cling to this recent concept.

Wherever an existing grammar school has been

transformed into a comprehensive school, difficulties have resulted from this. The average grammar-school teacher finds it extraordinarily hard to assume a larger role, and to accept the need to change his methods to meet the needs of the great majority of children. Parents can be misled by the name 'grammar school' into expecting for their children a kind of education which it may not be right for the school to give, and which it does not try to give. The terms 'high school' and 'grammar school', then, which in their Leicestershire connotation did not find favour with the Crowther Council, should perhaps be replaced by those familiar in America: junior and senior high schools.

Other two-tier proposals

Leicestershire is not the only county to consider adopting a two-tier system, though it has pressed on more vigorously than the others. *Derbyshire*, for example, while preferring the orthodox comprehensive school, is soon to develop some existing buildings as junior and senior high schools, with transfer probably at fourteen – though the exact relationship of the junior to the senior high school may be modified in the light of local conditions and local wishes.

At Hemsworth, in the *West Riding*, two districts are expected each to have a senior high school fed by a number of junior high schools. It is proposed to transfer *all* children at fourteen. In this way every child, regardless of his parents' desire or ability to keep him longer at school, will get at least a taste of the superior opportunities and more adult atmosphere of the senior school. Here is an exciting challenge to the staff. If they can work out suitable courses, and become as much youth leaders as schoolmasters and schoolmistresses, the two terms or one year they will have with many boys and girls could prove something of a magic touchstone: an invaluable period of preparation for the testing transition from school to work. It is likely, too, that a growing number will decide to stay until sixteen or later.

This straightforward system is also contemplated for other West Riding areas. It was, indeed, originally suggested for Ecclesfield by the divisional executive officer, Mr S. Wright, in 1957–8, but has not come to fruition there. Now that the case for raising the age for compulsory schooling to sixteen by 1970 (or earlier) is generally accepted, it is probable that transfer of all children at fourteen will be a common feature of local two-tier plans.

The most complete and detailed plan of all for two-tier reorganization has come from *Stoke-on-Trent*. In 1959 the education committee reviewed the situation, buildings, and accommodation of each secondary school in that large and difficult area, where much of the provision is inferior and out of date. It proposed not one solution but two alternatives, each of which had marked attractions.

Plan A was based on transfer at sixteen. It proposed the establishment of twenty-four high schools (eleven to sixteen), from which pupils desiring further education would go to one junior college (sixteen to eighteen-plus). The proportion likely to stay beyond sixteen was perhaps underestimated, and almost certainly, in view of the national trend and the special success of comprehensive schools in encouraging continued education, two such colleges would be needed. But this is a point of planning detail. Plan A offered new hope and higher status to existing 'modern' schools. In it the education of the over-sixteens could be thought of as something different from 'schooling'. The whole pattern, nevertheless, corresponded to the main framework of secondary education today, with its different approach to sixth-form work, organization, and attitudes.

Plan B looked rather to the independent-school sector

for inspiration. Realistically, it took account of the widely-varying standards of accommodation offered by existing schools. The smallest of these would have become lower (i.e. preparatory) schools for the two years eleven to thirteen. Such an organization has its precedents in many grammar schools and in some comprehensive schools. It offers the security of the smaller and more intimate community, and can be a valuable aid to the transition from primary to secondary education. (New Zealand has very similar intermediate schools from eleven to thirteen.) Other secondary schools would, like the 'public' schools, have operated from the age of thirteen upwards. They would have been common high schools, some with a three-year course (thirteen to sixteen), others with five-year courses (thirteen to eighteen). In ten cases, lower and common high schools would have been combined to form joint high schools (eleven to sixteen). Six of the common high schools were to carry G CE advanced level courses.

Both Stoke schemes, *A* and *B*, had exciting possibilities. Alas, reform works slowly in the world of the Potteries: a world of the 1930s still, rather than the 1960s. As Mervyn Jones has said in *Potbank* :[1]

The council, though it has a solid Labour majority, is not interested in comprehensive schools. The lucky ones in the eleven-plus go to the long-established grammar schools with no particular distinction on a national scale.

Here, as too often elsewhere in England, the fire and vision of the active few are frustrated not by the open, intelligent argument of supporters of selective schooling, but by the conservative section of a local party which might never have read – indeed, one suspects, perhaps never has read – the Labour Party's *Learning to Live*. The elected representatives, it seems, do not make the best use of the brains they can draw on. The quality of Stoke's thought

1. Secker and Warburg, 1961.

and planning, like the quality of its earthenware, is not matched by the vigorous enterprise needed to promote the production and sale of both kinds of goods in the bustling 1960s.

There is hope for the future. Longton High School is being developed as a sixth-form centre. Two comprehensive schools are developing from 'modern' schools which have had GCE courses. It is better than nothing – but what might have been!

Other abortive proposals for different versions of two-tier reorganization have been made in Rotherham and Carlisle. The idea is everywhere in the air, however, and the forces of reaction cannot hold the pass forever. In *Newcastle upon Tyne*, for example, reform is afoot. In 1958 the education committee decided to reorganize the city's secondary education on comprehensive lines. Apart from providing new comprehensive schools in new housing districts, a number of two-tier proposals have been made for the use of existing schools in established areas. These will be considered in due course.

A number of divisional executives (in *Middlesex*, for example, Wood Green, Twickenham, and Tottenham) have looked with favour on two-tier reorganization. Their plans, however, require the final approval of the county, which is the local education authority.

The first junior college to be set up by a local authority may be at *Mexborough* in the West Riding. It will provide for the nearby grammar school's sixth form, and also take those boys and girls over fifteen from 'modern' schools in the area who wish to continue their education. A new venture, too, is the independent international Atlantic College at St Donat's, in Glamorgan, for boys aged sixteen to nineteen. An earlier foundation doing the same kind of thing is the War Office's Welbeck College.

This may well prove the pattern towards which most

two-tier experiments will move. The growth of 'modern' schools, and in particular their development of GCE courses to ordinary level, has gone too far for the junior/senior high-school arrangement to be acceptable in many parts of the country. At the same time, the swelling of sixth-form numbers must compel grammar schools to concentrate increasingly and perhaps wholly on the work at this stage, which in fact they do best. In this way they will become an invaluable link between compulsory comprehensive education on the one hand and the tremendous diversity of voluntary higher education on the other.

Whatever the particular variant chosen, two-tier secondary education has three very practical virtues for us today.

First, it makes possible an early, rapid, and widespread change away from selection at eleven for different types of school and towards comprehensive education.

Secondly, it can be introduced by any local education authority without reference to the Minister at all, provided the opening, closing, or substantial enlargement of a school is not involved.

Thirdly, it facilitates and helps the public more readily to understand the main need in English secondary education. This is twofold: (a) extension of *common* education for two, three, or four years beyond the primary school, putting an end to premature selection, bias, and specialization; (b) its blossoming into the rich variety of *comprehensive* education in the later years – an education which takes full account of the wide range of individual differences, the great diversity of abilities, aptitudes, and ambitions, and yet (in its most complete form) provides for all these needs within the senior comprehensive school.

Lessons from Canada

Canada has had separate junior and senior high schools in

different provinces since 1927, as well as orthodox comprehensive schools. Until very recently this was the situation at South Peel, in Ontario. Compulsory schooling there ends at sixteen, but the normal junior high school age range (grades seven to nine) was twelve to fifteen, the senior, fifteen to eighteen. The less able pupils, however, usually either stayed at the 'junior high' to sixteen, or spent the last year in a technical school in nearby Toronto. Although the senior high school (grades ten to thirteen) was open to all who could progress beyond grade nine, in fact it tended to be mainly a school for the more able pupils. The similarity with Leicestershire is striking. South Peel has now, however, decided that in view of certain special local circumstances the unbroken comprehensive school (grades seven to twelve) is a better economic proposition for them. For this reason, rather than for purely educational ones, it is changing over to normal high schools.

At North York, a rapidly growing township of over 250,000 people in the metropolitan area of Toronto, the junior/senior high-school arrangement also exists, but it works very differently. The local authority does not favour keeping dull pupils aged fifteen-plus in an environment intended for younger children. Pointing out that they are often physically, socially, and emotionally very mature, perhaps more so than their intellectual superiors, the director of education, Dr F. W. Minkler, believes it is particularly important that they should all move into the senior high school for their final year. There they may continue to associate with their fellows of the same age, to their own benefit and to the advantage of the younger pupils left to run junior high school affairs. They can profit from the bigger and better range of vocational courses and workshop equipment available (and economically better able to be provided) in the senior high schools.

In North York it quite often happens that laggards thus

introduced to a more mature environment, who would otherwise have left the junior high school at sixteen, decide to stay longer at school and become better qualified. The North York system, in fact, closely similar to that proposed for Hemsworth in the West Riding, seems to possess the advantages of South Peel without the drawbacks. On a recent visit I found parents, teachers, and administrators very proud of this system and well pleased with its results.

Moving west through Ontario to British Columbia, where both two-tier and orthodox comprehensive schools are also common and well-tried, I found no agreement about their respective merits. I talked with Dr David Gaitskell, himself a former junior high-school principal, and cousin of our late Labour leader. He favoured the two-tier pattern. Others plumped for continuity of schooling throughout adolescence.

In favour of separate junior/senior high schools one hears three main claims:

1. The junior high school helps children to make a gradual transition from the all-purpose class teacher of the primary school to the many specialist teachers of the secondary school. At North York about two thirds of the first year timetable in the junior high school is taught by the form teacher, in the second year one third. In the third year, normal secondary-school specialist teaching obtains.

2. In the junior high school, boys and girls can remain boys and girls, and avoid the sophisticated influence of older pupils. They are happier, too, because they have a bigger say in the running of their own affairs; and the intimacy of the small community is particularly important during adolescence. In the same way, a senior high school is a more mature grown-up community, which older adolescents find more acceptable than an ordinary school.

3. A bigger range of optional courses can be provided in

a senior high school than in a 'through' school of the same size.

On the other side the main arguments are these:

1. A break after only three years is harmful. Some pupils take the better part of a year to adjust to their new teachers and the new environment in a senior high school. Continuity and undisturbed growth are essential in the education of adolescents.

2. It is the junior high-school boys and girls who at fourteen and fifteen are the most flighty and least responsible. They need the steadying influence and example of the seventeen- and eighteen-year-olds.

3. The standard of teaching and the personal quality of teachers in the junior high schools tends to be average and rather mediocre. The influence of the real scholar is needed, both among his colleagues and on the most gifted pupils.

The disagreement is not likely to end in victory for either side, in England or in North America. Both forms of organization are needed, according to different local conditions.

Sweden

The best example for the planners of a flexible system of comprehensive schools is perhaps that of Sweden. In 1950, after years of careful study, a great programme of educational reform was introduced. It is being implemented gradually, and may be complete by about 1970.

The essential feature of the Swedish plan is the basic three-year stage. Schooling begins at seven, and the stages are seven to ten, ten to thirteen, and thirteen to sixteen. There is no formal move from primary to secondary education, from one approach to another. The curriculum and the teaching of one stage blend into those of the next.

From the administrator's viewpoint this gradual build-up has great advantages. It means that, as Stoke envisaged in its Plan B, schools suited to different age ranges can be linked together in various patterns according to local circumstances. For example, there may be some schools providing for a double range, such as seven to thirteen or ten to sixteen. Occasionally, in a remote district, one might have one school for ages seven to sixteen. Such administrative flexibility requires agreement among teachers about certain basic work at each stage, for example the main ground to be covered in mathematics and science.

The Swedish reform has been made easier than similar reform in England by the fact that the Swedish *gymnasium*, or grammar school, normally covers the fifteen-to-nineteen age group only. For the present, common education runs to fifteen rather than sixteen, and beyond fifteen the paths diverge into academic, technical, and general courses.

A report by Torsten Husén and Nils-Eric Svensson, of the University of Stockholm, should encourage English scholars to make similar comparative studies.[1] In 1954 comprehensive schools were introduced on the south side of Stockholm while two types of secondary school were retained on the north side. Full records were available to indicate the social class from which all the children aged ten-plus came, and the whole of this age group took tests of their intelligence, attainment, and attitudes to future schooling. Since that time, Husén and Svensson have been re-testing samples of the original age group.

Their first (provisional) conclusions after two years 'run counter to the opinion held by many educators, at least in Sweden, that it is the able children who are most

1. *The School Review* (University of Chicago Press, Spring 1960), pp. 36–51, 'Pedagogic Milieu and Development of Intellectual Skills'.

handicapped by being taught in undifferentiated classes'. They say that: 1. on the south side of the city, the kind of children who would previously have gone to the *realskola* (academic school) have not suffered from being in a comprehensive school: their progress is similar to that of comparable children in *realskola* on the north side; 2. children from poorer homes have responded most strongly to the superior advantages of the comprehensive school over the Swedish equivalent of the 'modern' school: there is nothing to be said for grouping together children of average and below-average capacity.

No break at eleven?

England's break at eleven between primary and secondary education is the product of administrative convenience. It was recommended by the Hadow Committee in 1926 because, with compulsory school ending at fourteen, nothing less than a three-year course could justify the creation of separate senior schools, although psychological theories then current were invoked, as they were later in the 1940s, to give a proper aura of 'expertism' to the new line.

Today the current of public opinion swings strongly away from early specialization, and this helps the cause of those who would prolong primary education to thirteen instead of eleven. But there is no guarantee that such an extension will *in itself* prevent early specialization. The independent preparatory schools' normal age range is from eight or nine to thirteen or fourteen. In fact this means an extension downwards, to the age of nine, of the kind of academic studies normally begun at eleven in a local grammar school.

With this *caveat*, there is something to be said for reshaping the maintained school system on the lines of the independent system, i.e. five to nine; nine to thirteen; thirteen to eighteen. It would dispense with the very early break between infant and junior schools which we have now at the age of seven; in the middle school it would facilitate a more gradual transition from class teacher to specialist; and it would enable the present secondary schools to make room for and concentrate more effectively on the increasing number of pupils who are staying beyond fifteen. A big comprehensive school of 2,000 would not only be cut to 1,200 but it would be a more efficient and attractive place; and there is little doubt that its special rooms and equipment would still be fully exploited.

However, if the old idea of 'primary' and 'secondary' stages were to give way to a more flexible pattern of schools, a new Education Act would be necessary, and opinion generally is not yet ready for this. The main structure of the 1944 Act rests on the concept of three distinct successive stages: primary, secondary, and further education.

My review of some significant developments at home and abroad is not intended to be at all complete. Its main purpose has been to show the flexibility of structure which is possible and perhaps desirable in comprehensive education. It is simply not true to say that, unless the Government permits the large-scale building of new schools, nothing can be done to put an end to the eleven-plus, and all it stands for. If local authorities are sufficiently determined and energetic they can make their own change-over forthwith by converting 'modern' schools into junior high schools, and grammar schools into either senior high schools or sixth-form colleges.

Public education is urgently needed on this issue. The facts should be made widely known, the pros and cons thoroughly debated in every city and county. Parents will then realize that, far from 'destroying' the grammar school, we are proposing a still more vital role for it; that far from lowering scholastic standards, comprehensive schools (whether one-tier or two-tier) are likely to raise them; and that instead of restricting opportunity, they enlarge it. The matter calls in fact for effective communication – effective teaching. For professional educators, that should not be too difficult.

5. A Programme for Progress

A BOOK on comprehensive schools should not use the title at all if it does not, however unworthily, at least attempt to view the subject in a truly comprehensive way. For comprehensive secondary schools as we know them today are after all little more than excrescences on the established social and educational system. Such an organization has yet to be accepted *in practice* by any of the three main political parties. Labour has preached the gospel since it went out of office in 1951, but in most of the local areas which it controls it has notoriously failed to implement the comprehensive principle. Yet, as I have shown, this is perfectly feasible without the consent of the Minister of Education.

Even where a comprehensive pattern is being established, what is happening inside the schools? Are liberal ideas about the equal worth of all men, which inspire the movement towards the comprehensive schools, being translated into more democratic social structures? Into broader, more wise and human teaching of world history and sociology? Into more careful psychological guidance of each pupil, greater collaboration between teachers and parents? Here and there, yes; but not commonly, or more than tentatively. This is not to belittle the heroic achievements of the pioneers, whose first job it was to prove that the schools were successful by the traditional standards which the public understood. This they have amply done.

But we cannot be content with that. Indeed, if a comprehensive system came into being which merely hotted up the individual struggle for power, the rat-race for social prestige, it might be better that the reform had never been begun. As a historian I am realist enough to consider this outcome more than a possibility. And yet – man's age-long struggle towards better things, inching his way along like a worm in the soil, proves too that we must each contribute our pitiful little best to this end in our own way, if life is to have any purpose at all. No one who reads this book will ever see the end of the road. All we can hope to do is first to understand the problem, secondly to create our own vision of the right solution, and thirdly to work towards it with all the good means in our power.

I almost wrote 'all means in our power'. But history is full of misguided men and women who, believing that the end justified any means, in the long run damned themselves and their cause by their ruthless actions: Cromwell at Drogheda ... the men of the Inquisition ... Stalin ... And in more subtle ways, too, reform inspired by unworthy motives, achieved by secret negotiation and pressures, itself becomes tainted. The ambitious, dictatorial Morant[1] stands as a warning to all educational administrators.

What we, as a people, must resolve is that proposals for important changes must be made public long before any decision on them is taken, with ample time allowed for public debate; that full consultation with parents, teachers, and governors should always precede a local authority's decision to go ahead. This does not mean that elected representatives should abandon their right and duty to make the final decision, even an unpopular one; only that all points of view should first be heard. Morally there is everything to be said for free and open persuasion, nothing at all for the secret *coup*. Why fear the light, if our cause is just ? *Magna est veritas et praevalebit.*

Independent schools

At the beginning of this book I compared England's three-

1. Sir Robert Morant, Permanent Secretary to the Board of Education, 1903–11.

class educational system to a three-lane athletics track with no staggered start. On the inside lane run the favoured six per cent who attend independent and semi-independent (direct-grant) schools.

What are their advantages? First, independent schools have distinctly smaller classes than the schools run by local authorities. In L.E.A. primary schools in January 1961, there were twenty-nine pupils per teacher, and 80,000 of the 128,000 classes had from thirty to fifty pupils in each. Grammar schools were only slightly better off: there were eighteen pupils per teacher, but 11,000 of the 24,000 classes had more than thirty pupils. Comprehensive schools had nineteen pupils per teacher, and just under half of the 4,931 classes had more than thirty pupils.

The picture in recognized independent schools is very different. There, the pupil-to-teacher ratio in nursery schools is ten, in primary schools twelve, in schools which are primary-cum-secondary fifteen, and in secondary schools twelve. The sizes of their classes are not given, but can be deduced. In all the maintained primary and secondary schools of England and Wales there are 289,000 teachers, including allowance for part-timers, and the pupil-to-teacher ratio is twenty-four. In all recognized independent schools the corresponding figures are 23,000 teachers, and a ratio of thirteen. There are other independent schools, not yet recognized as efficient, whose average number of pupils per full-time teacher is worse (eighteen); but this category will gradually be eliminated.

Why should independent schools have such material advantages in staffing? One reason is, quite simply, that these schools are prepared to spend more money on teachers than are the Government and local councils. Independent governing bodies tend to believe that teachers are important: more important than buildings and equipment, though they do not despise these things. Where fees and funds permit, they will not only engage a good many more teachers than a local authority school would be allowed to have, but will even pay them more than the national (Burnham) scale.

Parents endorse this line. More and more queue up to pay the ever-rising fees which such a policy requires. Fees at Eton are now £500 a year; at Millfield School, Somerset, up to £750; at Heathfield, the exclusive girls' school attended by Princess Alexandra, £480; at Roedean £417. Some members of the Government and the civil service who each year pare the estimates for national expenditure on education may well at the same time be signing big cheques for the education of their own children or grandchildren at independent schools. This applies to Labour as well as Conservative M.P.s and voters, though the proportion of the former is much smaller.

The danger is clear. Men and women whose children are withdrawn from the old bare buildings of the local primary school, from the strain and hazards of the eleven-plus examination, from the overcrowded classes of the 'secondary modern', are likely to lack some of the urgency which compels reform. Without a doubt, the most valid and powerful argument for bringing all independent schools into the State system is that it would bring the young Mac-millans, Hailshams, Gaitskells, and Bonham-Carters into the local classrooms. The chance of early vigorous action to wipe out the black spots in national education would be transformed overnight.

Teachers, too, are quite rare creatures now; there are not nearly enough of them. To prevent attractive resorts like Brighton and Bournemouth enticing more than their share from Birmingham and Bootle, the local authorities observe a rationing scheme – the kind of scheme we found fair and necessary with food, clothes, building materials, petrol, and so on during the 1940s. But in the war years the rich citizen was not legally allowed to buy more than his fair share. Today he can do just that in education, on average buying the services of twice as many teachers for his son at an independent school as a poor man's child will get at a local school.

The power of the purse, used in such a way, must be ended. It sins against natural justice. In the long run, moreover, it is a time-bomb under the independent schools themselves which could eventually lead to their total abolition.

Two reforms are needed at once. They would require legislation, but the 1944 Act has already shown the way by requiring the Ministry of Education to inspect and register independent schools. The first is that all independent schools should conform to the corresponding L.E.A. pupil-to-teacher ratio, with a reasonable allowance of extra staff for boarding schools, whether independent or in the State system. The second is that all schools, independent and maintained alike, should pay salaries only according to the Burnham scale, with deductions for benefits such as residence. If a school's reputation and atmosphere attract highly-qualified men, well and good; but the rich school should not steal the cream of talent from either the poor independent school or the local authority's school by the chink of money alone.

Of course, a period of at least ten years would have to be allowed to enable the relatively over-staffed schools of Eton and Harrow, Winchester and Millfield, to adjust to the new 'fair shares' order without hardship to individual teachers. Even so, the change would bring not insignificant results. A committee set up by the National Union of Teachers has calculated that 'the recruitment of the 500,000 privately-educated children to L.E.A. schools would require up to 25,000 more teachers, but well over 30,000 would be released from the independent schools. In the U.K. as a whole, 6.5 per cent of the children were fee-payers in 1959, but 9.0 per cent of the teachers taught them.'[1]

When these changes are agreed, England will be able to look less passionately at the idea and practice of independent schools. Much could be and has been written, erudite and entertaining, attractive and alarming, about what goes on inside them and what they stand for. The public schools have had their internal as well as external critics, from Alec Waugh[2] to John Wilson.[3] In 1958, a righteously indignant Labour Party roared its denunciation.

This system [it thundered] distorts the choice of people for responsible positions; it damages national efficiency and offends the sense of justice. Further, it creates an irrational social cleavage which is a great injury to education as a whole ... All members of the Labour Party, and indeed all who desire equality of opportunity and social justice, will agree that the existence of this privileged sector of education is undesirable.[4]

But what did it then propose to do about this terrible state of affairs? Nothing whatever. A later conference took a more positive line, but by that time decisions of Labour conferences had ceased to matter as they once did.

The purely educational benefits given by an orthodox boarding school are overrated. Boys and masters live an unnaturally restricted life in a closed, almost monastic community. All the enlightened cultural pursuits that can be devised do not produce the freedom to be either sociable or alone, to be part of the busy life of one's neighbourhood, to belong to home instead of being a stranger in the holidays, that a good day school ensures. The life of the boarding school, in relation to the world of the late twentieth century, is exclusive; that of the day school inclusive. The

1. *Investment for National Survival* (N.U.T., 1959), p. 26.
2. *The Loom of Youth*, 1917.
3. *Public Schools and Private Practice*, 1962.
4. *Learning to Live.*

fact that the Russians have espoused boarding-school education, with its great potential for conditioning its products, is not necessarily a recommendation.

The essential fact is that the 'public' schools, despite grave limitations, are socially pre-eminent because they are the places where our rulers used to be educated, and by and large still are. Moreover, personal contacts with Oxford and Cambridge colleges still ensure them an undue proportion of places at our leading universities. In November 1961, two out of every three Cabinet ministers were old boys of 'public' schools, particularly of Eton; so were two thirds of the bishops and the justices, and half of the top civil servants. Forty years back, headmasters like Rendall of Winchester made no bones about their aristocratic faith, their belief in leadership by a privileged élite; forty years on, will the message have changed?

Many 'public'-school heads would like to revive the proposal of the Fleming committee that they should recruit a minority of their pupils from local schools. If this were to come about, they would naturally try to select boys of quality – of character if not of brain – who could readily be absorbed into and indeed strengthen the society to which they were admitted. Their gain would be the local schools' loss. The class system, once more revised and reinvigorated, would be more firmly established than ever.

English independent schools fall into three main groups, which are poles apart. Within them, however, individual differences are usually outweighed by the resemblance.

First in prestige and influence are the so-called 'public' schools, some 200 in number, whose heads are members of the Headmasters' conference. The real leaders are the bigger, independent boys' boarding schools such as Eton, Harrow, Winchester, Rugby, Clifton, and Charterhouse. A few, like St Paul's, are day schools. Girls' 'public' schools are fewer in both number and influence on national life.

The left wing of this powerful group is represented by such schools as Bryanston, Abbotsholme, and Gordonstoun. These are moderately progressive, with a reputation for *not* worshipping games and for encouraging liberal opinion, tough physical effort, and sometimes unorthodox teaching methods. Basically they derive from the Boy Scout era, but the choice of Gordonstoun for Prince Charles will doubtless ensure for them an Indian summer.

The second main group, small in number and in patent influence, but yet of real significance in the underflow of educational ideas, is that of the coeducational 'progressive' schools. The most radical and best known is Summerhill, creation of A. S. Neill, a Scotsman who revolted against the thin-lipped puritanism of John Knox still embraced by so many of his countrymen – perhaps in guilty expiation for their quite contradictory worship of Robby Burns. Neill's ideas are essentially in tune with those of great radical thinkers like Rousseau and Dewey, great teachers like Homer Lane and David Wills.

Neill, more than anyone else, has swung teachers' opinion in this country from its old reliance on authority and the cane to hesitant recognition that a child's first need is love, and with love respect for the free growth of his personality: free, that is, from the arbitrary compulsion of elders, and disciplined instead by social experience. The magic of the inspired reformer is there in Neill's books, in his talks to teachers, who still flock to hear him, above all in the absolute sincerity which marks his own school community. Teachers may soon forget high-sounding principles, but they remember the loveless girl who stole again and again; the girl to whom, on each occasion, Neill gave threepence, and after a particularly big theft fourpence – to prove to her, the *sine qua non* before he could begin to help further, that regardless of what she did he was on her side. Today's friendliness between pupil and teacher is probably the greatest difference between the classrooms of 1963 and those of 1923. The change owes much to Neill, and to others in independent coeducational schools who have practised similar principles.

Yet had independent schools been prohibited in 1923, would Neill ever have been allowed to do, unhindered, what he needed to do? Freedom in education is a first requirement for the establishment and maintenance of a free society. It must be preserved. This means, however, more than an absence of controls; it means having the wherewithal to live freely: money.

Industry has already given substantial sums of money to certain independent schools, but a general allocation to all the needy and worthy is required. This can only be provided by the nation as a whole. A fund administered by an independent body, quite detached from the Ministry of Education, may be the only practicable arrangement. It will work so long as we as a people favour liberal principles; and if we lose them, freedom inside or outside the State system of schools will not survive.

The third main group of independent schools is a mixed bag of minor boarding schools (preparatory and secondary) and small independent day schools, usually for younger children. Too many of these exist because of social snobbery, a desire that 'nice' children shall not mix with street kids and learn naughty words, rough accents, and bad manners. (These same parents go dutifully to church to pay their respects to the memory of a man whose personal example was that of mixing with the riff-raff.) Other parents choose them because they want the advantage of small classes for their children, and are prepared to buy these superior conditions, though in the long run this is done at the expense of other children.

I have urged that independent schools should be preserved, but that material privileges should not be bought there. With this provision enforced, we may expect most of the unworthy schools to wither away. What we ought not to destroy is the distinctive character, perhaps the spiritual atmosphere, of schools with a truly educational purpose. The freedom of Summerhill and Dartington is matched by the Anglican worship of Clifton, by Catholic Stonyhurst, Quaker Ackworth, and Methodist Kingswood. All have their special contributions to make to a free, classless, diversified, creative society. None of these schools should choose, or I think would choose, to gather to itself only the most able, the naturally favoured children. Each should be a mixed comprehensive community, taking children who for one reason or another cannot have a normal home and school upbringing.

In sum, we need to weed out the worst of the independent schools, to keep and in some respects reform the best. That done, independent schools – along with aided schools of similar foundation – will become a necessary part of a full system of comprehensive education. Without them a free society would be incomplete.

Schools for the community

Home is the baby's world. For all other members of the family, however, it is not sufficient in itself, though essential as a fount of love and security. Both children and parents need a much richer, more varied social life than modern homes – little brick huts in lonely suburban streets – can give. In each neighbourhood we need not only people sharing a whole range of occupations, but as much as possible the places where those occupations are carried on. The segregation of 'residential areas' from factories, shops, and offices betrays an abysmal ignorance of social psychology.

At the same time we must make the best of the actual situation today. We have to recognize that the need for a planned extension of educational facilities is made more urgent by the cultural poverty of the urban and suburban street, and by the latter's lack of communal life. In this situation we cannot overlook the example of Peckham. Between 1926 and 1950 the Pioneer Health Centre at Peckham, one of the inner suburbs of south-east London, showed in impressive fashion what could be done.

The Peckham centre had a medical wing, swimming bath, gymnasium, canteen, theatre, library, and a range of rooms which could be adapted for different social activities. It also had its own nursery and primary school. Membership was limited to whole families from the immediate neighbourhood – the distance that a woman could push a pram. It was essentially an experiment in the positive promotion of social health, in the enrichment of the physical and cultural life of a mixed community; and it ended, ironically enough, when this formerly self-supporting centre, hit by steeply rising costs after the war, failed to get financial support from a Labour government pledged to the advancement of social welfare.

Its example remains, though no community centre so complete has yet been developed elsewhere. The need for a stronger link between school and home at the primary stage is particularly important.

Nursery-infant schools are wanted, for they help enormously to widen a child's social experience. There he is safe, busy, and happy. The school can provide play material specially designed for his use. The teachers are trained to understand his needs. Above all, in these days of small families, he has there the companionship necessary for his proper social and emotional development.

Instead of full-time schooling from five to six as at present, the young child needs to be initiated gradually into the exhausting social life of school. At the same time there is no doubt that a great many four-year-old children are fretfully at a loose end while at home. The sensible answer is to introduce half-time schooling for all children between the ages of four and six. It would make no extra demands on either our buildings or our supply of teachers. By local arrangement, and taking into account as far as possible mothers' preferences, each child would attend school either in the morning (9.30–12 noon) or the afternoon (1.30–4.0). Some children would stay for school dinner after the morning session, others would come for it before the afternoon session. More would have dinner at home, but the extra age-group would probably mean that the total having school dinner aged from four to six would not differ very much from the number aged five to six who now have it.

School should not, however, be a means of taking the child *from* the mother or of relieving her of responsibility. We are paying far more than an economic price for the labour of married women. We pay with the neglect of small children while mother and father are away from home, with insecurity and personal and social instability. One supports both people's need for a higher standard of living and the need of most married women for a fuller social life. Yet if we really believe that proper attention and security in early childhood are essential for later happiness and the prevention of delinquency, we ought to forbid the *full-time* employment of mothers whose children are under six years old, at least; and we should bear the economic consequences. If history is any guide at all, necessity would produce the appropriate solution – most probably a speeding-up of automation.

It would of course be wrong and futile to do no more than order women back to the kitchen. The necessary complement is to develop our primary schools as social and education centres for children *and mothers*. They could be very simple versions of Peckham. Attached to the school would be a small branch of the county library, with books and magazines of special interest to mothers. The weekly clinic would be held in a suitable room on the premises. An attractively furnished canteen-cum-common room could be run by the staff who provide school dinners; indeed, any further use of existing capital plant (in this case the kitchens) should always be welcomed as contributing to greater efficiency and economy. Talks and discussions could be arranged occasionally in mornings or afternoons for mothers whose children were in school at the same time. This is an idea which Townswomen's Guilds, Women's Institutes, and Mothers' Unions might well consider.

Something of the kind is already being done at the City of Leicester Training College. Each Wednesday morning more than a score of local mothers bring their children of pre-school age, including babies, to the nursery-infant department of the college. Students look after the children while mothers play tennis, keep fit on the trampoline, study flower arrangement, or paint. Experts from big stores give talks on such topics as fashions and make-up. The local health visitor may talk about child management. These mothers greatly value their visits.

Such a solution would seem to take account of all the main points which at present cause us concern: the need to initiate young children gradually, instead of frightening them by pushing them in off the deep end; the need to enlarge and enrich the social life of young mothers, without driving them away from their families to factory, office, or shop; the need to divert our growing national wealth to the areas of society where its support is most needed; and finally, the very practical need to achieve these reforms without making any extra demands on the already insufficient supply of teachers, and with a minimum of extra building.

We should then look forward to a ten-year period of full-time comprehensive schooling for everyone, from six to sixteen. In what stages this should be organized is not in itself of the first importance. In practice, the disposition of buildings as a result of the 1944 decision to have primary and secondary education in two stages, with transfer between ten and a half and twelve, settles the issue as far as most local education authorities are concerned. That would mean primary education from six to eleven in the existing primary or junior schools and secondary education from eleven to sixteen in the existing 'modern' schools.

Some local authorities, however, might prefer to have infant schools from four to eight (the first two years being half-time), junior schools from eight to twelve (the age first decreed by the 1944 Act for transfer from primary to secondary education), and secondary schools from twelve to sixteen or eighteen. Another alternative is to have three-year cycles of development: four to seven, nursery/infant stage; seven to ten, one class-teacher for nearly all subjects, as at present; ten to thirteen, gradual introduction to some specialization, with no more than three or four teachers altogether taking any one class; and thirteen to sixteen, secondary education as now understood, with biases growing from a common core. The child's moving at this age or that is not important, so long as his progress through a comprehensive curriculum up to sixteen follows a broad pattern which is generally accepted. National agreement on basic courses and methods, though not in other matters, is becoming necessary as more people move about the country.

Throughout this period, right through from six to sixteen, our schools must be ready to feed and provide for children's special interests as they emerge. We should reject any notion of a completely uniform curriculum which would put them all in a strait-jacket. There are precious talents of language and music, art and drama, for example, which will sometimes require extra time; and in the later years, at least, a boy or girl may have good reason to drop some subject or subjects and to concentrate more thoroughly on others. Just as emphatically, we must stop forcing children to choose one subject to the exclusion of another, before they want or are ready to make that choice.

The question is often posed: should a school prepare a pupil to fit into existing society or to change it? For me the choice does not arise. Society will change in any case – all living things do. The important question is: in what direction should it change? It is not for any schoolmaster to provide the answer. His job is to help his pupils to open their minds, to gain the experience from which in due course they will be able to think out their own answers.

For that reason I believe the comprehensive school, a school which sets out more specifically than any other to provide for a complete community, should have a special concern to educate its pupils for active participation in a free democracy. It can only do this by letting them work and live in a society which is as democratic as the law of education and the incomplete maturity of the pupils per- mit. Such a qualification must leave room for considerable disagreement about what is possible and desirable, and it would be wrong for any conservative-minded teacher to budge from his principles. Sincerity on his part ensures security for the child. Nevertheless, it should be observed that there have been many schools practising a much greater degree of democracy than is common in England's new comprehensive schools. In this sphere, as in the de- tailed work of the classroom, Rowe is showing in an Essex 'modern' school what can be done.

The principal need of modern democracy is not that we should pick or train a class of leaders whom the rest can

follow with unquestioning loyalty, but that we should
spread responsibility much more widely and encourage
intelligent discussion and active participation in councils
and committees by everyone. Enlargement must replace
selection, socially as well as in the curriculum.

Each group situation will produce its own Admirable
Crichton to take charge when required, provided an offi-
cially-appointed élite does not already sit in the seat of
power. There should be many groupings of various sizes
within a school. A small group can act as a whole. When it
is too large to do this, authority can often be delegated *ad
hoc* for particular purposes to different people. In this way,
every boy and girl receives some training in democratic
procedure, and a large proportion of them are likely to
hold executive office for a time. The extension of personal
experience is essential to the effective working of a democratic system. We want all, not only a favoured or ambitious few, to become active citizens in the future.

Why do so many heads, of all types of school, hesitate
about this vitally important aspect of the social education
of their pupils? Some, perhaps, are not well informed of
experiments elsewhere, and it does not occur to them to
adopt any system other than that to which they have been
accustomed. There may be an element of caution; it is
easier and safer to appoint your own agents than to risk
having to work with individuals appointed by others, and
of whom you may not approve. Moreover, it greatly
strengthens a headmaster's hand to wield this power of
patronage. 'All power corrupts . . .' and where is the tyrant
who has voluntarily become a constitutional monarch?
It is easier and more efficient to take decisions quickly than
to await the laborious processes of committees – especially
when you know the answer much better than they. 'Democracy only rates two cheers', as E. M. Forster observed,
even with the man in the street. It can hardly be expected

to evoke an eager welcome from the average headmaster's chair. Education in democracy requires the guidance of mature, relaxed, patient men and women, who are not plagued with subconscious doubts about themselves, the children, or the rightness of the policy they are carrying out.

The secondary schools, whether their age range be eleven to sixteen, eleven to eighteen, or any other variant, have a job to do which extends far beyond the classroom and the individual pupils. I have suggested that the primary school should be a social and educational centre for children and mothers too. But the family does not cease to exist when childhood gives way to adolescence. Marriage-guidance counsellors tell us that marriages are most in danger after the first ten years. Every member of the family, mother and father, boy and girl, feels the pressing call for a fuller, more satisfying life than the ordinary home can possibly provide by itself. The cleavage of each from the others is not uncommon, yet Peckham showed that it need not happen.

The secondary school which serves the whole local community is the nucleus around which a rich and happy neighbourhood life can be built. It must be more than a school: rather, a community college on the Cambridge-shire and Leicestershire models. It should be a centre of local culture, entertainment, and recreation. Its premises should be available to whatever societies may spring up. There must be games rooms, comfortably furnished common rooms, playing fields, library, and all the appurtenances of a civilized and very diverse community of people. Not least of the dividends will be the recognition that the school is but part of a larger whole, that parents belong there too, that the whole business of education is a matter for consultation among the interested parties – parents, teachers, adult tutors, committee members, and so on. A

Dr Busby would hardly be an appropriate appointment for the wardenship of such a democratic institution.

The grammar school's future role: the sixth-form college

What of the sixth form? It is important that at this stage, with academically minded pupils and teachers, we retain the attitudes of scholarship which distinguish the best grammar, comprehensive, and independent schools. The two last-named types of school have exploded the fallacy that these attitudes can only be created with a segregated academic élite. The comprehensive schools are already attracting increasing numbers of sixteen-to-eighteen-year-olds who want courses which, whether general or geared to future careers in industry or commerce, must be quite different from those of the Oxbridge scholarship hunter.

There are powerful arguments in favour of providing for the older adolescent in separate sixth-form colleges. Support for this arrangement, first canvassed during the 1940s, has slowly gained ground. Croydon is returning to the idea mooted in 1954. In fact, the armed forces have been first in the field here. Now comes the first independent Atlantic College, and the Mexborough experiment. More are sure to follow.

The advantages of the sixth-form college are these. First, such a community, of moderate size (say 200–500), can yet economically and efficiently offer a more varied programme than that available in the vast majority of grammar- and comprehensive-school sixth forms. Expensive advanced equipment can be provided, in the knowledge that it will be fully used. Highly-qualified specialist staff will likewise be employed to maximum advantage.

Tiny sixth-form classes are costly in staffing. Even in a school of 1,200 like Holyhead, different years of the sixth form have to be taught together. The local education authority recognizes that the alternative to starting a sixth-form college is to make the schools even larger than they are now.[1] The sixth forms of Anglesey have increased from 125 in 1953 to 211 in 1961. The island is compact, and a central college at Llangefni for 200–300 students would be a perfectly practical proposition.

Secondly, it would be possible in such a college to treat the pupils as students, giving them a bigger share in the running of their own community than is normally possible in school. They would feel that they had left school behind, and the prospect of meeting and working with sixth-formers drawn from other schools would be an attractive one. We need to widen adolescent horizons, not restrict them. It may be felt that the idea of 'staying on at school' is irksome to many, particularly sixteen-year-old girls, and that the routine duties of patrolling corridors and keeping younger children in order are not very impressive forms of training in responsibility. As others leave, the sixth-former may feel that he is becoming a bigger and bigger fish in an ever-dwindling pond.

In the college, on the other hand, he would mix with many more sixth-formers from a variety of schools. This would enlarge his social experience and give him a different sort of responsibility, akin to that of the university undergraduate. Indeed, I feel that sixth-formers are ready for the degree of self-government usually accorded to university students today, and that the latter in turn ought to be treated much more like adults than fledglings.

In some rural areas, houses for weekly boarders would be necessary. The experience would do many country children a world of good. In their late teens they need to get away more than they do from their rather isolated homes. This gentle easing of the bonds would be a valuable experience.

Thirdly, although some grammar schools let their brighter

1. *Education*, 23 February 1962, pp. 366–9.

pupils by-pass the ordinary-level examinations of GCE and go on to specialist sixth-form work early, the great majority of schools still prefer to give a general education to fifteen or sixteen and put their pupils in for a broad range of ordinary-level subjects. This is partly because parents, pupils, and teachers like to have an external guide to the pupil's best future course of study; but it is also a partial guarantee against premature specialization.

Beyond the ordinary level of GCE, teachers commonly adopt a different, a tutorial approach to their pupils. This is the best feature of grammar-school education; and in many places, as the demand for higher education spreads strongly, the logical arrangement would be to ask an existing grammar school to concentrate increasingly and eventually wholly on sixth-form work with students aged fifteen or sixteen to eighteen-plus. There is an excellent precedent in Sweden's *gymnasium*, with its fifteen-to-nineteen age range. This would, for example, be a logical and attractive next step in Leicestershire, where senior grammar schools for thirteen- or fourteen-year-olds to eighteen-year-olds are over-full, while junior high schools, at present doing only the groundwork for GCE up to fourteen, yet keeping about half their pupils to fifteen, are perfectly capable of providing for all up to fifteen or sixteen, including ordinary-level work. Croydon plans to do this from the start.

By this arrangement those pupils who leave at fifteen or sixteen, and they are the majority, can take a leading part in their school's affairs to an extent impossible while they are overshadowed by sixth-formers. There will be no break in the secondary schooling. The brightest pupils could take GCE at ordinary level after four years, or by-pass it altogether and go on to the college at fifteen. It is a prospect to which both grammar and 'modern' schools, the latter already developing GCE courses and becoming increasingly comprehensive, can reach forward. Here is the assurance of a place in the sun that both of them need and deserve.

The fact is that schools, like the people of whom they are composed, tend to grow up. The grammar school's normal age range was at one time eight to sixteen. Since the war it has become eleven to eighteen. It is realistic to ask 'modern' and grammar schools to stop pretending that they are equal and parallel and to start functioning end-on. At the same time it would be foolish to set a target which could not be hit in the foreseeable future, such as the general development of efficient sixth forms in 'modern' schools, for which generations of children would pay a heavy price in the years between.

There are of course many who hold that there should be no break in secondary schooling. They believe that sixth-formers set a good example to the younger children, that some stay on at their present school who would not go to a separate college, that studies to advanced level should run on unbroken from at least thirteen to eighteen. Where, after long and serious consideration, teachers and parents prefer the 'through' school system to the two-tier system, and such schools exist or can be provided, their views should of course prevail. Only by experience and unhurried comparison can the pros and cons of this debate be thoroughly understood and properly weighed.

The comprehensive county college

So far I have said nothing about the people who will still leave as early as sixteen even when compulsory schooling is extended for an extra year. Crowther held out only the most distant hopes of the introduction of part-time county colleges for those aged from sixteen to eighteen; yet since 1944, in theory and in statute, we have recognized the need to extend educational guidance to eighteen for everyone. The 1944 Education Act prescribed county colleges which would give compulsory education for one day per week for forty-four weeks in the year, or, with rural districts in mind, one term of eight weeks or two terms of four weeks each. The Crowther council felt that this must come after the raising of the leaving age. Meanwhile, it encouraged the extension of day-release courses at colleges of further education. Between 1970 and 1980 it was hoped to have five years' experience with compulsory part-time attendance in a few chosen areas, followed by its gradual extension over the whole country.

There are three ways in which educational guidance for all between sixteen and eighteen might be provided. One is in separate colleges for part-timers only, as envisaged in the 1944 Act. In practice this would prove very difficult, and the practical snags explain why we have shied away from tackling the problem. It would be hard to find yet more sites for educational buildings in urban centres, although the new wave of redevelopment there does give some opportunity. Further, the total number of pupils the staff of such a college must handle is too great, as we know from the experience of existing day-continuation colleges like Bournville and Boots. Four hundred students a day means 2,000 a week – far too many for the staff to get to know well; yet close personal knowledge and influence are more important than anything else to teenagers. Nor is it easy to see how staff of the high calibre necessary would be recruited for such work alone.

The second possibility is that part-time education from sixteen to eighteen should be given wholly or mainly in colleges of further education, as it often is now. There is much to be said for this while day release is voluntary. The adult atmosphere appeals; there is greater freedom than in school, but it is tempered by the influence of older students, and by established standards of work and social conduct. Certainly the School for General Studies at Ipswich's magnificent Civic College is most successful. It has well over 400 full-time students, drawn from secondary schools and admitted without examination on the head teacher's recommendation. A wide range of subjects is offered to the ordinary and advanced levels of GCE. Some students go on to universities and training colleges, others stay at the Civic College and qualify in art, engineering, building, clerical and secretarial work, and so on. It is a complete alternative to the grammar-school sixth form. On the other hand, numbers under a *compulsory* system would be so high that teenagers might tend to dominate everything, and many of the staff in further-education colleges have no particular interest in or experience of handling adolescents.

The third possibility is the comprehensive county college for all aged from fifteen or sixteen to eighteen-plus. This would be a development of the process for which I have reasoned already; the transformation of the grammar school into a school or college for older adolescents, at first, perhaps, from thirteen or fourteen, later from fifteen or sixteen, to eighteen-plus.

We are already finding that comprehensive schools have to provide for a new type of sixth-former – the boy or girl who is not at all academic. To this extent the cleavage between students and others is blurred, and socially this is all to the good. But the parting of the ways between the scholar, the professional man, and the educated technician on the one side, all of whom are in future likely to stay at school to eighteen, and the unskilled or semi-skilled young worker on the other, who leaves at sixteen or earlier, is still sharp. They take different roads into adult life, and it is in late adolescence that impressions burn deepest. There is a very real danger that, despite comprehensive schooling to sixteen, this sharp divergence of experience and interests thereafter will undermine at least some of the good foundations laid earlier; and that in later life, class differences and lack of mutual understanding will be almost as strong as ever they were.

The new kind of sixth form in comprehensive schools is the first sign of a familiar historical process. A higher range of education for older pupils, first appreciated by the wealthy and the able, is gradually coming to seem desirable to more and more of the working class. This process will go on; but as we go down the scale of natural ability, higher secondary education will have to include a considerable amount of practical work. Such work must be realistic – and where better can a good apprenticeship be given than in an up-to-date factory or office? One can foresee the development of very close links between the sixth-form college and industry, just as in a different sphere one can expect much closer collaboration between college and school in the training of teachers.

The Russians are beginning to realize the importance of mixing studies with practical work in the later teens. We too are questioning excessive specialization, and feeling the need to develop rounded people, whole men. More time is being spent by intellectual sixth-formers on arts and crafts and technical jobs. Leicester's Gateway School is a splendid example of this. The trend will continue. As it does, the distinction between continuing one's education and going out to work will fade. More and more pupils will opt for the former when it is seen as a realistic all-round education with a vocational point to it. It has always had such a point for the future lawyer, teacher, or administrator; we shall merely be extending it to the more varied needs of all members of society.

It does not take any great effort of the imagination, then, to visualize the sixth-form college of the future as pretty comprehensive in the range of activities it offers and the range of ability it attracts. It will be staffed by some of the most gifted personalities in the teaching profession, men and women who by achievement and character can win the regard of critical sixteen- to eighteen-year-old pupils. Its academic prowess will ensure high prestige in the community at large. Economically it will be the soundest of propositions, by intensive use fully justifying first-rate staffing and equipment.

What could be simpler and more natural than that, in the fullness of time, the voluntary growth of these colleges should be completed by the government's helping hand? If we began some such colleges in 1965, it is probable that by 1975 they would be attracting more than half the sixteen-to-eighteen age group. It may well be, then, that instead of the cumbersome arrangements which formal compulsory part-time education would always require, the really practical answer will lie in the process with which we are already familiar: the voluntary extension of education, clinched in due course by the government's compulsion, to ensure that the children of poor or obtuse parents are not left for ever out in the cold. So we should simply have compulsory education extended first to seventeen, and ultimately perhaps to eighteen.

The great difference between past and future extensions, however, must be this. In the past we have talked, rightly, of 'raising the school-leaving age'. In future we must speak of 'college education for all'. The new phrase implies near-adult status and freedom, and optional courses of study. It implies, too, a very flexible administration which will make it possible for some students to have four days at their books and one in the workshop, others four days in the factory (a good well-run one) and one at their books, and others again varying proportions of study and practical work in between those extremes.

Of course we need a national overhaul of apprenticeship systems. A survey in December 1961 by the Institute of Youth Employment Officers showed that many employers misuse the term 'apprenticeship' and fail to provide adequate training. The concept of apprenticeship is a splendid thing, but the time has come for it to be placed firmly under the wing of the local education authority. Grants in lieu of wages might well be made to students who chose to attend the college beyond sixteen – an excellent and just way of helping the desired development in the early, voluntary stage.

The term 'sixth form' is too limited and inappropriate for an institution of the kind I have been describing. 'Junior college' would be even more patronizing and inept. The sensible term would surely be simply 'county college': dignified and pleasing to the ear, and symbolic of the importance of our local education authorities in the national system of education. Its part-time connotation is already something of a dead letter.

I have already suggested that this county college can best evolve from the grammar school of today, by our giving the latter the honoured place of responsibility for all higher secondary education in an end-on pattern. It would be the final link in a fully comprehensive chain: final, that is, as far as we can usefully peer into the future now. Some day, no doubt, we shall have comprehensive universities.[1]

The real future of the comprehensive idea does not, then, lie in the comprehensive secondary school as it is at present understood. It has been an invaluable pioneer, experimental, intermediate institution. The schools of Leicestershire, taking us further on the way, must in turn develop, or hand over the torch. Given the will, we could shape all

1. 'I see great advantages in a vision, maybe twenty years hence, of comprehensive universities for all those desirous of education after eighteen whatever subject they are taking.' A. T. Bourne-Arton, Conservative M.P. for Darlington (*Northern Echo*, 10 January 1962).

our existing schools into a vigorous, national, comprehensive system by 1970. Infant classes or school half-time from four to six; primary school from six to eleven; secondary school from eleven to fifteen or sixteen; county college from fifteen or sixteen to eighteen-plus: this is a framework which many, perhaps most, authorities could best introduce, and the one which I personally favour most. But it need not be standard and invariable. We might, for example, have stages four to eight, eight to eleven, eleven to fourteen, fourteen to eighteen; or five to nine, nine to thirteen, thirteen to eighteen, according to local circumstances.

The teachers

Comprehensive education does more than open the doors of opportunity to all children. It represents a different, a larger and more generous attitude of mind. For forty years we have been too preoccupied with the mere *measurement* of ability; with testing and grading, with selection and rejection and allocation. Many teachers and administrators have almost come to regard this classification as their main job. Worshipping at an altar bearing the mystic symbol 'IQ', set up by a priesthood of pseudo-scientists called 'psychometrists', they have sometimes seemed to forget the age-old power of teaching, and the capacity of a child to keep on growing and learning – when it is put in the right environment.

Now our teachers, in all types of school, are beginning to turn from the false gods, to concern themselves less with the arid assessment of a child's inborn ability and idle predictions about its future ceiling, and more with nourishing all the diverse talents children have. I say, deliberately, that this is a fresh approach – not a new approach: for it is truly a rebirth of learning, not a revolution in education. Those who protest so vigorously against present trends, and describe them as an assault on traditional values, need a historical perspective which goes a little further back than War Office selection boards.

If the comprehensive schools are to take full advantage of the reforms which are afoot in the framework of our system, they need above all broad-minded scholarly teachers who see themselves as friends and counsellors rather than as circus-masters, who rely on timely advice and encouragement rather than the superficial incentives of the whip and the carrot. If we turn back the pages of history we can often catch a glimpse of what first-class teaching quality can do.

From 1796 to 1833 Richmond School, Yorkshire, had only from fifty to sixty boys each year; but under a great scholar and master, James Tate, five or six went every year to either Cambridge or Oxford. Half of them took Firsts; no less than thirteen of 'Tate's Invincibles', as they were called, were elected fellows of Trinity, and more became fellows elsewhere. Such was the pride and confidence of Richmond in its little school that every year, when the Cambridge tripos results were due, the whole town turned out, gathering round the Market Cross to await the coming of the carrier up the Great North Road with his news of yet more triumphs.[1]

But the Tates, the Thrings, the Arnolds are all too rare; and with less-gifted masters Richmond faded into obscurity. Today, while we rejoice in the 'ups', we cannot afford to contemplate such 'downs' as overtook our forebears in the eighteenth and nineteenth centuries. We need a high and constant level of competence to sustain the brilliant; and that means training. If university standards of scholarship and quality are to pervade our comprehensive schools,

1. L. P. Wenham, *The History of Richmond School, Yorkshire* (Herald Press, 1958).

both primary and secondary, it can only be done through our university institutes of education.

We have today a deeply divided teaching profession. Only one teacher in three in maintained secondary schools is a graduate; only one in twenty-five in maintained primary schools. In recognized independent schools the corresponding figures are four out of five and one in three. To more than four out of five of all teachers in maintained schools, university scholarship is a closed book; and they have never experienced the rich variety of contacts with able minds geared to widely different interests. Their world has been the comparatively narrow world of the training college – a world of teachers and would-be teachers only, with its legacy of inferior conditions and staffing ratios, an out-of-date relic of the old elementary system.

Is it possible for an all-round improvement in the general education of our people to be achieved, if the mental nourishment and stimulation of teachers themselves is to be cramped in this way? It is not enough to modify and improve training-college conditions, important and desirable as are the steps being taken to this end.

Equally unacceptable is the argument that most primary teachers and some secondary teachers are unsuited to an academic university course. This overlooks the pre-war position, when it was common to have in our universities men whose ability and attainments were no greater than those of most of the students now in training colleges; yet they gave much to the life of the university community and gained much from it.

Perhaps it assumes that university teaching methods are and always will be dry, unimaginative, and incapable of relating theory to practice and personal experience in a stimulating way. This is not true. At Leicester (and I am sure the same applies to other universities) the School of Education frequently experiments with new approaches and techniques, and each year it trains a group of graduates from its own and other universities to teach in primary schools.

The truth is that only the best education is good enough for the teachers of the prosperous society that will be the Britain of the future, a Britain relying more than ever before on trained intelligence for its prosperity. That means a university education now for all who can profit by it; and ultimately, as overall standards steadily rise, for all teachers.

The day must come, and the sooner the better, when all graduates who wish to teach in school are required first of all to train. It would, however, be a great mistake if we followed Scotland in taking the professional education and training of teachers out of the universities, instead of seeking integration the other way by bringing it all in. The Scottish 'colleges of education' are still conscious of their inferior status *vis-à-vis* the universities, and many concerned with their work and government now favour their incorporation in neighbouring universities. I have recently observed this process of integrating training colleges in the universities of Canada at different stages in different provinces, and I am convinced that it is both right and feasible. The new 'college and faculty of education' must be regarded as roughly equivalent in size, and fully equal in status, not to another department (e.g. of history, or classics, or botany) but to the faculty of arts, or science, or social science, or medicine.

It is essential, at the earliest possible moment, to require all graduates who wish to teach to train for the job. It is also necessary to encourage those training-college students who wish and are suitably qualified to read for a degree, to do so. A third development most urgently needed, particularly for the increasing number of students who are taking general degrees, is the recognition in all our universities of

'Education' as one of the subjects which may be taken in a three-year or four-year course for the first degree. This last step, desirable on academic grounds, would also take much of the increasing load off the one-year post-graduate departments.

Such expansion would not necessitate a lowering of standards. Only students with an approved qualification would be admitted to degree courses; but there are clearly going to be many more of these. What is not so readily seen, however, is that a *further* advance in the quality of the work done by schools will then become possible, provided their staffs have themselves experienced the challenge of working in the richest of all educational environments. It will take time – perhaps twenty years – to bring all suitable training colleges into and up to the universities, and to attain the ideal of a graduate profession. That is the best of reasons for early action; but it must be action in the right direction.

I have suggested earlier that the comprehensive school should be deeply concerned to help to shape and transmit a communal culture, rich and diverse as the colours of rainbow silk, whose essentials all members of a liberal, democratic society can recognize and share. This task is impossible so long as our teachers are themselves sharply divided into what are in effect two classes, graduate and non-graduate, with their different backgrounds and correspondingly different social status and public esteem. The ending of this cleavage is one of the major reforms necessary for the effective development of a system of comprehensive education.

Conclusion

'Nothing,' said Victor Hugo, 'is so powerful as an idea whose time has come.'

The arguments against our divided system of education

mount higher day by day. Parents are no longer content to accept the verdict of mental tests at eleven as authoritative. In the county of Leicester, for example, they overwhelmingly oppose absorption by the city in a revision of boundaries, for one prime reason: they fear a return to the eleven-plus examination. Discontent over the eighteen-plus bottleneck, which stems from the same restrictive attitudes among those in power, will become still more vocal.

In examination results, comprehensive schools are already turning the tables on those who raised alarm about the threat to academic standards. Despite the serious handicaps imposed on them, these schools are beginning to suggest that it is the segregated system whose performance may be inferior. The self-important moguls of education, who take for granted the inferiority of the mass of their fellow men, cling to their mean gloomy belief in a limited pool of ability, as though the human mind were something static. In fact its capacity for growth is written large on the pages of history. Our pioneer comprehensive schools, and I include the new two-tier schools under this term, are nobly adding to that story.

Their continued success, which I confidently expect, will produce a growing flood of young people eager to continue their studies beyond the secondary stage. With the early achievements of these schools in mind, I presented to the Home Universities Conference in 1958 a case for expanding the number of university places in Britain from 124,000, the target then accepted by the University Grants Committee, to a minimum of 170,000 by 1966. The realization of this figure, which was subsequently accepted by the Association of University Teachers and by the University Grants Committee, has been postponed by the Government, which aims merely at 150,000 by 1967 and 170,000 by 1973–4. This is plainly inadequate.

Looking further ahead, it is impossible to put any ceiling to future expansion. The process of education is self-perpetuating, and the whole record of history indicates that increased opportunity begets ever-increasing response.

At a time when man's resources are greater than ever before, we correspondingly need to think big, to recapture some of the fire and vision of giants like H. G. Wells, Bernard Shaw, Gilbert Murray, and W. T. Stead. 'Moral eunuchs', Stead called those who were afraid to put right what all the evidence showed to be wrong. The term, scathing as it is, would not be out of place in some parts of the education service today. So far we have barely scratched the surface of necessary reform. Today's experiments are but stumbling footsteps on the long road to universal education, which, as Wells prophesied, will be 'organized upon a scale and of a penetration and quality beyond all present experience', and give 'a yield beyond comparison greater than any yield of able and brilliant men that the world has known hitherto'.

Large changes in the framework of our educational system are required, but in themselves they can do no more than make good education possible. They simply get us to the starting-gate. What matters most of all is what goes on inside the schools.

It is very important that our comprehensive schools shall not content themselves with merely achieving equal opportunity for the competitive success of individual pupils. In the years ahead, now that the folly of eleven-plus segregation is everywhere being recognized, they will be tempted of the devil. They will be shown and offered all the scholastic kingdoms, including Oxford and Cambridge, York and Canterbury. Tempting though such prizes are, they must not be allowed to divert the new schools from their larger purpose: the forging of a communal culture by the pursuit of quality with equality, by the education of their pupils in and for democracy, and by the creation of happy vigorous, local communities in which the school is the focus of social and educational life.

English society in the sixties is far from noble or inspiring. But man is not a helpless creature. It is up to us to direct new forces in the way we believe to be right. 'How much is still alive in England!' cried Carlyle. 'How much has not yet come into life!' But a promise, too, is there: 'The centuries are big; and the birth-hour is coming, not yet come.'

List of Schools
broadly comprehensive in character
in England, Wales, and the Isle of Man,
1962

Schools are coeducational unless shown as boys' or girls'. The denomination of voluntary aided schools is shown in brackets. The year in which the school assumed its present broadly comprehensive character, whether as a new foundation or not, is given in front of the name of the school. The approximate number of pupils on roll follows the name.

I have included (a) schools which take all the pupils of the district, regardless of numerous variations in their internal organization, and (b) schools which, though they do not at present take all local pupils, are fully equipped to do so.

The total number of schools listed is 239, distributed as follows: English Counties 71; London 68; English County Boroughs 52; Welsh Counties 40; Welsh County Boroughs 4; Isle of Man 4.

ENGLAND: COUNTIES

Buckinghamshire	1958	Warren Field, Slough (1,200)
Cornwall	1962	Sir James Smith's, Camelford (470)
Cumberland	1957	Samuel King's, Alston (160)
	1959	Millom (1,160)
Derbyshire	1957	Westfield (1,050)
Devon	1959	Tavistock (1,140)
	1961	Plymstock (680)
Dorset	1956	Alfred Colfox, Bridport (900)
	1959	Gillingham (730)
Durham	1958	Wolsingham (1,110)
Essex	1959	North Romford (950)
	1962	Harlow Burnt Mill (370)
Gloucestershire	1952	Newent (625)
	1952	Tetbury (450)

Herefordshire		1962	Lady Hawkins, Kington (600)
Hertfordshire		1955	Ashlyns, Berkhamsted (1,100)
Lancashire	Kirkby:	1956	Brookfield (1,800)
		1960	Ruffwood (1,650)
		1960	St Gregory's (girls) (R.C.) (1,600)
		1960	St Kevin's (boys) (R.C.) (1,650)
Leicestershire		1947	Humphrey Perkins, Barrow-on-Soar (870)
	Birstall:	1960	Longslade Grammar (490)
		1960	Stonehill High (660)
		1960	Hamilton High, Scraptoft (630)
		1962	Roundhill High, Thurmaston (775)
	Hinckley:	1957	Hinckley Grammar (770)
		1957	Hastings High, Burbage (810)
		1957	Heathfield High, Earl Shilton (670)
		1957	Mountgrace High (girls) (500)
		1957	Westfield High (boys) (500)
	Wigston:	1957	Guthlaxton Grammar (1,140)
		1957	Abington High (530)
		1957	Gartree High, Oadby (770)
		1957	South Wigston Boys' High (480)
		1957	South Wigston Girls' High (460)
		1959	Bushloe High (530)
Middlesex		1948	Mellow Lane, Hayes (1,110)
		1952	Mount Grace, Potters Bar (1,400)
		1959	Convent of Jesus and Mary, Willesden (girls) (R.C.) (920)
Oxfordshire		1949	Burford (640)
		1954	Chipping Norton (620)
Shropshire		1950	Bishops Castle (450)
Staffordshire		1955	Regis, Tettenhall (1,140)
		1955	Willenhall (870)
		1956	Tividale (900)
		1957	Ounsdale (940)

Suffolk, West	1958	Sudbury (girls) (700)
Surrey	1957	St Andrews, Leatherhead (girls) (R.C.) (360)
Sussex, West	1958	Thomas Bennett, Crawley (1,580)
	1960	Hazelwick, Crawley (1,020)
	1960	King's Manor, Shoreham (girls) (740)
Warwickshire	1952	Nicholas Chamberlaine, Bedworth (1,680)
	1952	Dunsmore Girls', Rugby (670)
	1958	Dunsmore Boys', Rugby (700)
Westmorland	1948	Windermere (boys) (275)
	1955	Kirkby Stephen (400)
	1959	Appleby (425)
Yorkshire, East Riding	1948	Withernsea (1,020)
	1960	Hessle (1,000)
Yorkshire, North Riding	1951	Easingwold (730)
	1957	Thirsk (680)
	1958	Lady Lumley, Pickering (670)
Yorkshire, West Riding	1950	Calder (1,225)
	1956	Colne Valley (1,750)
	1956	Penistone (1,125)
	1957	Tadcaster (1,365)
	1958	Settle (550)
	1959	Elland (1,020)
	1961	Swinton (1,375)
	1961	Wombwell (1,080)
	1962	Aston Woodhouse (1,760)

ENGLAND: LONDON

Battersea	1946	Battersea County (1,200)
Camberwell	1946	Peckham (girls) (1,500)
	1957	Thomas Calton (1,100)
	1958	Collingwood (girls) (1,000)
	1958	Kingsdale (1,850)
	1958	Peckham Manor (boys) (1,400)
	1958	William Penn (boys) (1,650)
Deptford	1956	Samuel Pepys (boys) (900)
	1957	S.E. London (boys) (850)
Finsbury	1960	Risinghill (1,200)

Fulham	1955	Henry Compton (boys) (1,000)
	1956	Hurlingham (girls) (1,350)
	1961	Gilliatt (girls) (900)
Greenwich	1954	Kidbrooke (girls) (2,000)
Hackney	1958	Edith Cavell (1,150)
	1960	Brooke House (boys) (1,000)
	1960	Clapton Park (girls) (1,000)
	1960	South Hackney (1,000)
	1960	Upton House (950)
Hammersmith	1957	Christopher Wren (boys) (1,400)
	1957	Hammersmith County (girls) (1,250)
Hampstead	1961	Hampstead (600)
Islington	1955	Holloway (boys) (1,300)
	1956	Barnsbury Girls' (1,100)
	1957	Tollington Park (1,250)
	1958	Barnsbury Boys' (1,150)
	1959	Archway (950)
Kensington	1958	Holland Park (2,150)
	1958	Isaac Newton (boys) (700)
	1958	Ladbroke (girls) (750)
Lambeth	1955	Dick Sheppard (girls) (1,050)
	1956	Tulse Hill (boys) (2,150)
	1957	Vauxhall Manor (girls) (1,050)
	1958	Norwood (girls) (800)
	1960	Kennington (boys) (1,100)
	1960	Stockwell Manor (1,450)
Lewisham	1955	Catford Girls' (1,050)
	1956	Forest Hill (boys) (1,450)
	1956	Sydenham (girls) (1,750)
	1957	Catford Boys' (1,250)
	1957	Sedgehill (1,650)
	1958	Churchdown (girls) (800)
	1959	Malory (1,300)
Paddington	1957	North Paddington (1,000)
	1960	Rutherford (boys) (650)
	1961	Sarah Siddons (girls) (900)
St Marylebone	1956	Kynaston (boys) (850)
St Pancras	1949	Haverstock (1,650)

	1956	Parliament Hill (girls) (1,300)
	1959	Acland Burghley (1,000)
	1959	Sir William Collins (boys) (1,000)
Shoreditch	1958	Shoreditch (1,300)
Southwark	1946	Walworth (900)
	1961	Trinity (girls) (1,150)
Stoke Newington	1955	Woodbury Down (1,250)
Wandsworth	1955	Mayfield (girls) (2,000)
	1956	Elliott (2,000)
	1956	Wandsworth (boys) (2,000)
	1957	Spencer Park (boys) (1,250)
	1958	Garratt Green (girls) (1,950)
	1958	Southfields (1,000)
	1959	Bishop Thomas Grant (R.C.) (950)
	1959	Ensham (girls) (1,250)
	1960	Hillcroft (boys) (1,350)
Woolwich	1956	Eltham Green (2,100)
	1958	Crown Woods (1,850)
	1959	Abbey Wood (900)
	1961	Bloomfield (boys) (900)

ENGLAND: COUNTY BOROUGHS

Birmingham	1955	Great Barr (1,700)
	1955	Sheldon Heath (1,920)
Bradford	1961	Buttershaw (900)
Bristol	1954	Hengrove (1,000)
	1954	Lockleaze (1,100)
	1955	Ashton Park (1,000)
	1955	Bedminster Down (1,120)
	1955	Brislington (1,130)
	1955	Henbury (1,470)
	1956	Speedwell Boys' (720)
	1956	Speedwell Girls' (700)
	1957	Monks Park (1,320)
	1957	Withywood (1,270)
	1959	Greenway (boys) (750)
	1959	Lawrence Weston (850)
	1959	Pen Park (girls) (730)
	1960	Hartcliffe (840)
	1962	St Bede's (R.C.) (300)

Bristol – *contd*

	1962	St Bernadette (R.C.) (660)
	1962	St Thomas More (R.C.) (570)
Coventry	1954	Caludon Castle (boys) (1,480)
	1954	Woodlands (boys) (1,520)
	1955	Lyng Hall (girls) (1,120)
	1955	Whitley Abbey (1,160)
	1956	Coundon Court (girls) (780)
	1956	Foxford (1,270)
	1957	Tile Hill Wood (girls) (660)
	1959	Binley Park (920)
Darlington	1960	St Mary's (boys) (R.C.) (450)
Leeds	1956	Foxwood (boys) (1,550)
	1958	Allerton Grange (1,550)
	1961	Matthew Murray (1,100)
Liverpool	1949	Blue Coat (boys) (C. of E.) (420)
	1958	Gateacre (1,600)
	1958	King David (Hebrew) (550)
	1961	St Francis Xavier's (boys) (R.C.) (290)
Manchester	1960	Plant Hill (1,050)
	1960	Yew Tree (1,300)
Newcastle	1960	Kenton (1,180)
Nottingham	1958	Fairham (boys) (1,400)
Reading	1960	Ashmead (boys) (800)
Sheffield	1960	Myers Grove (615)
Southend-on-Sea	1945	St Bernard's Convent (girls) (R.C.) (750)
Stoke-on-Trent	1962	Blurton (1,000)
	1962	Willfield (960)
Walsall	1961	T. P. Riley (1,100)
West Bromwich	1955	Churchfields (1,850)
West Ham	1945	St Angela's (girls) (R.C.) (810)
	1945	St Bonaventure's (boys) (R.C.) (800)
	1961	The Deanery (girls) (840)
Wolverhampton	1956	Highfields (1,170)
	1956	Northicote (875)

WALES: COUNTIES

Anglesey	1949	Holyhead (1,260)

Anglesey – *contd*

	1953	Sir Thomas Jones, Amlwch (830)
	1953	David Hughes, Beaumaris (825)
	1953	Llangefni (990)
Breconshire	1954	Maesydderwen, Ystradgynlais (850)
	1955	Brynmawr (770)
	1955	Builth Wells (370)
	1955	Cefn Coed (520)
Caernarvonshire	1950	Dyffryn Ogwen, Bethesda (500)
	1950	Dyffryn Nantlle (560)
	1951	Ysgol Botwnnog (420)
	1954	Eifionydd (575)
Cardiganshire	1947	Lampeter (520)
	1949	Tregaron (400)
	1951	Aberaeron (650)
	1959	Cardigan (780)
Carmarthenshire	1958	Llandovery (460)
Denbighshire	1953	Dinas Bran, Llangollen (700)
	1961	Brynhyfryd, Ruthin (850)
Flintshire	1956	Ysgol Uwchradd, Y Rhyl (380)
	1957	Maelor (310)
	1959	Blessed Richard Gwyn (R.C.) (480)
	1961	Ysgol Uwchradd, Yr Wyddgrug (150)
Glamorgan	1956	Cynffig (900)
	1958	Sandfields, Port Talbot (1,510)
Merioneth	1949	Towyn (480)
	1954	Festiniog (580)
	1957	Harlech (600)
	1962	Dolgellau (300)
Monmouthshire	1946	Rhymney (675)
Montgomeryshire	1945	Llanfair (300)
	1945	Machynlleth (360)
	1946	Llanfyllin (430)
	1947	Llanidloes (370)
	1957	Newtown Boys' (420)
	1957	Newtown Girls' (410)

Pembrokeshire   1955   Fishguard (800)
                                     1958   Preseli (600)
                                     1958   St David's (350)
                                     1961   Greenhill, Tenby (800)

WALES: COUNTY BOROUGHS

Newport   1958   Duffryn (1,250)
                                     1958   Hartridge (1,300)
Swansea   1961   Mynyddbach (girls) (1,260)
                                     1961   Penlan (boys) (1,420)

ISLE OF MAN

                                     1946   Douglas Boys' (1,030)
                                     1946   Douglas Girls' (920)
                                     1946   Ramsey (560)
                                     1948   Castle Rushen (460)

Suggestions for Further Reading

Education Act, 1944 (H.M.S.O.).

Ministry of Education Pamphlet no. 1: *The Nation's Schools – their plan and purpose* (H.M.S.O., 1945).

Ministry of Education Pamphlet no. 9: *The New Secondary Education* (H.M.S.O., 1947).

The London School Plan (Staples, 1947).

Secondary Education: a report of the Advisory Council on Education in Scotland (H.M.S.O., 1947).

(ed.) Düring, I: *The Swedish School-Reform* (1946 School Commission, Uppsala, 1951).

Early Leaving: a report of the Central Advisory Council for Education (England) (H.M.S.O., 1954).

Simon, B.: *The Common Secondary School* (Lawrence & Wishart, 1955).

Arvidson, S.: *Education in Sweden* (Swedish Institute, Stockholm, 1955).

Pedley, R.: *Comprehensive Education: A New Approach* (Gollancz, 1956).

Rawson, W.: *The Werkplaats Adventure* – an account of Kees Bocke's great pioneer comprehensive school, its methods and psychology (V. Stuart, 1956).

Campbell, F. C. : *Eleven Plus and All That* – the grammar school in a changing society (Watts, 1956).

Floud, J. E., Halsey, A. H., and Martin, F. M.: *Social Class and Educational Opportunity* (Heinemann, 1956).

(ed.) Vernon, P. E.: *Secondary School Selection* – a British Psychological Society inquiry (Methuen, 1957).

Lester Smith, W. O.: *Education – an introductory survey* (Penguin Books, 1957).

(ed.) Simon, B.: *New Trends in English Education* (MacGibbon & Kee, 1957).

Gilkes, A. N.: *In Defence of Independent Education* (Gollancz, 1957).

(ed.) National Union of Teachers: *Inside the Comprehensive School* (Schoolmaster Publishing Company, 1958).

Equality in Education (Victory for Socialism, 1958).

Learning to Live (Labour Party, 1958).

Adams, A. L., and Miller, A.: *Opportunity in Education* (Liberal Publications Department, 1958).

Young, M.: *The Rise of the Meritocracy* (Thames and Hudson, 1958; Penguin Books, 1961).

(ed.) Andrews, J. H. M., and Brown, A. F.: *Composite High Schools in Canada* (Committee on Educational Research, Faculty of Education, University of Alberta, Edmonton, 1959).

Conant, J. B.: *The American High School Today* (McGraw-Hill, 1959).

15 to 18: a report of the Central Advisory Council for Education (England) (Crowther Report) (H.M.S.O.; vol. I, 1959; vol. II, 1960).

Lowndes, G. A. N.: *The English Educational System* (Hutchinson, 1960).

Chetwynd, H. R.: *Comprehensive School – the Story of Woodberry Down* (Routledge & Kegan Paul, 1960).

Rowe, A. W.: *The Education of the Average Child* (Harrap, 1960).

Miller, T. W. G.: *Values in the Comprehensive School* (Oliver & Boyd, 1961).

Furneaux, W. D.: *The Chosen Few* – an examination of some aspects of university selection in Britain (Oxford University Press for the Nuffield Foundation, 1961).

✕ *London Comprehensive Schools*: a survey of sixteen schools (London County Council, 1961).

Jackson, B., and Marsden, D.: *Education and the Working Class* (Routledge, 1962).

Neill, A. S.: *Summerhill – a radical approach to education* (Gollancz, 1962).

JOURNALS

Educational Research (Newnes for the National Foundation for Educational Research).

Forum: for the discussion of new trends in education (PSW Educational Publications, 71 Clarendon Park Road, Leicester).

Annual Reports of the Ministry of Education and Statistics of Education for England and Wales (H.M.S.O.).

A Glossary of Educational Terms

ALL-AGE SCHOOL: A school containing children of all ages from five to fifteen; those of secondary age will have failed to qualify for a grammar or technical school.

BILATERAL SCHOOL: A secondary school with two distinct sides: grammar/technical; or grammar/'modern'; or technical/'modern'.

COMPREHENSIVE SCHOOL: A school taking practically all the children from a given district (i.e. all apart from the educationally subnormal, the physically handicapped, and those attending independent schools) and not organized in distinct sides. The maintained primary schools of England and Wales (normal age range five to eleven) are thus comprehensive primary schools. The term 'comprehensive school' is, however, more usually applied to secondary schools which take practically all local school children aged eleven to nineteen. Recently it has been more loosely used, e.g. in the Crowther Report and by the London County Council, to indicate schools which provide suitable courses for a wide range of ability but which do not necessarily take practically all local children.

COUNTY COLLEGE: An institution to be provided by a local education authority under the 1944 Education Act, for compulsory, part-time attendance by young people under eighteen who are not in full-time attendance at a school or other educational institution. No county colleges have yet been provided. A broader concept has been suggested by the present author in *Comprehensive Education: A New Approach*, and in the present work.

DAY RELEASE: The arrangement by which employers allow certain workers time off without loss of pay, usually for one day a week, to study at a college of further education.

DIRECT-GRANT GRAMMAR SCHOOL: A school which is not under the control of the local education authority but which receives a financial grant direct from the Ministry of Education. This grant is at present £43 a year per pupil below the sixth form and £124 in the sixth form. To qualify for grant, the school must provide free places, to the extent of at least twenty-five per cent of its intake, to pupils who have spent at least two years in a maintained primary school. The school charges fees to other pupils, who may be admitted to the school's own primary department from the age of seven-plus.

DIVISIONAL EXECUTIVE: An *ad hoc* body for a particular district set up in accordance with the 1944 Education Act to deal with the day-to-day administration of primary and secondary education, and some aspects of further education, within the framework of the overall policy laid down by a county council, from which its delegated powers are derived.

ELEMENTARY SCHOOL: Before 1944, elementary education – concentrating very largely on the 'three Rs' (reading, writing and arithmetic) – was provided by voluntary bodies or by designated local authorities for children aged from five to fourteen who did not attend the fee-charging secondary schools.

ELEVEN-PLUS: The examination and selection procedure used by a local education authority to find a basis on which to allocate children leaving primary schools about the age of eleven to different types of secondary education.

EXCEPTED DISTRICT: Where the town council of a borough or urban district is designated as a Divisional Executive, this area is described as an Excepted District. Excepted Districts usually have rather more powers delegated from the county council than has an ordinary Divisional Executive.

FURTHER EDUCATION: Education for people who have left school. The official term does not include universities.

GENERAL CERTIFICATE OF EDUCATION (GCE): A certificate awarded as the result of a national examination, set by any one of eight examining boards. A candidate – who need not be attending a school – may sit for any number of subjects. There are no age restrictions, but in schools the Ordinary level is customarily taken about the age of sixteen in from one to ten subjects, and the Advanced level about the age of eighteen, in from one to four subjects.

GRADUATE TEACHER: A teacher holding a university degree. A graduate is regarded as a qualified teacher even though he may not have taken the optional one-year training course for the Graduate Certificate in Education. If, however, a graduate takes this training course and fails, he loses the teaching qualification which he had before he embarked on the course.

GRAMMAR SCHOOL: A secondary school providing a mainly academic course from eleven to sixteen or eighteen. It is the main route to the universities and the professions. Grammar schools maintained by local education authorities are of three kinds:

    1. *County schools* entirely provided by the L.E.A.

2. *Voluntary-controlled* schools originally provided by a voluntary body such as a church, but now entirely financed and controlled by the L.E.A., which supplies two-thirds of the school's governing body.

3. *Voluntary-aided schools* originally provided by a voluntary body which still maintains the fabric of the building but which relies on the L.E.A. for all running expenses. The L.E.A. supplies one-third of the governing body.

HIGH SCHOOL: In America, a comprehensive secondary school. The term is sometimes used in this sense in England, but it is also often applied to a girls' grammar school.

INDEPENDENT SCHOOL: A school which receives no money from public funds, and which therefore charges fees and may also have private endowments. All independent schools must be registered with the Ministry of Education and conform to prescribed minimum standards. In addition, schools may apply for inspection by Her Majesty's Inspectors in order to be 'recognized as efficient'.

IQ: 'Intelligence Quotient', or a child's intelligence rating compared with the average for his age and expressed as a percentage (the average being 100). It is determined by specially devised 'intelligence tests'.

LOCAL EDUCATION AUTHORITY (L.E.A.): The county council or county borough council responsible for providing and administering primary, secondary, and further education in its area.

MAINTAINED SCHOOL: A school provided, controlled, or aided by the local education authority.

'MODERN' SCHOOL: A maintained secondary school for children not selected for grammar or technical schools.

MULTILATERAL SCHOOL: A secondary school with three or more distinct sides, e.g. grammar, technical, and 'modern'. There is now only one multilateral school in England and Wales.

PREPARATORY SCHOOL: An independent school, age range usually between seven and fourteen, which prepares boys or girls for entry to 'public' schools *via* the Common Entrance examination (for independent schools) taken at thirteen.

PRIMARY EDUCATION: Education up to the age of about eleven, covering nursery schools or classes (two to five), infant school or department (five to seven), and junior school or department (seven to eleven).

'PUBLIC' SCHOOL: The term is not capable of exact definition,

but it is most commonly applied to the bigger or more famous
independent boys' boarding schools, about eighty in number,
whose heads are members of the 200-strong Head Masters' Conference. The less well-known schools whose heads are members
of H.M.C. are usually referred to as 'minor public schools'. A
'public' school is not public in any normal sense: it is not maintained by public funds, nor is it open by right to the children of
the public.

SECONDARY EDUCATION: Education from about eleven to fifteen (the end of compulsory schooling) and upwards to a normal
limit of nineteen-plus. Before 1944, however, it was not as now
the second main stage in education, but a superior type of education for some children (mainly fee-payers) aged seven to eight-
teen, organized separately from elementary education.

SETTING: Re-grouping of the classes of a given year into 'sets'
of roughly equal ability for a particular subject.

SIXTH FORM: The upper section of a secondary school, normally entered at fifteen or sixteen after taking some subjects at the
Ordinary level of GCE, and preparing for Advanced level in from
one to four subjects. Some pupils also prepare for university
scholarships. Comprehensive schools are increasingly in their sixth
forms providing courses in non-academic subjects.

SPECIAL SCHOOL: A school for children who are physically or
mentally handicapped.

STREAMING: Grouping of the children of each year's intake
into classes according to their general ability. Thus ninety children
would be divided into three classes of thirty each: A (above
average); B (about average); C (below average).

TECHNICAL SCHOOL: A secondary school giving a general
course with a technical bias up to sixteen or eighteen. Commonly
takes the second layer of general ability, as indicated by the
eleven-plus examination, after the top layer has been selected
for grammar schools. There are few technical schools in England
and Wales (228), and the number is declining. The Ministry's
present policy is to provide technical education in both grammar
and 'modern' schools.

TRAINING COLLEGE: A college for the training of teachers,
mainly or entirely non-graduate teachers aged eighteen or over,
who study for three years for the Certificate in Education. Minimum admission qualification is a pass in five subjects at the
Ordinary level of GCE. Colleges are grouped under University
Institutes of Education (except at Cambridge, where the Institute

is not a university body) which exercise a general supervision over their work and award the Certificate (or Graduate Certificate) in Education.

TRIPARTITE SYSTEM: An ugly phrase for an ugly arrangement: the division of secondary education into grammar, technical, and 'modern' schools.

Index